PENGUIN PASSNOTES

The Mayor of Casterbridge

Dominic Hyland was born in 1935 and educated at St John's College, Cambridge, where he read English. Following this he gained three postgraduate qualifications in education. He has taught in secondary and further education and is currently working with the Open University and the University of Liverpool He is Chief Examiner in English Literature for one of the largest examination boards in the country, and was formerly Chief Examiner in the Use of English.

PENGUIN PASSNOTES

THOMAS HARDY

The Mayor of Casterbridge

DOMINIC HYLAND
ADVISORY EDITOR: S. H. COOTE, M.A., PH.D

PENGUIN BOOKS

Penguin Books Ltd, Harmondsworth, Middlesex, England
Viking Penguin Inc., 40 West 23rd Street, New York, New York 10010, U.S.A.
Penguin Books Australia Ltd, Ringwood, Victoria, Australia
Penguin Books Canada Limited, 2801 John Street, Markham, Ontario, Canada L3R 1B4
Penguin Books (N.Z.) Ltd, 182–190 Wairau Road, Auckland 10, New Zealand

First published 1984
Reprinted 1986, 1987

Made and printed in Great Britain by
Richard Clay Ltd, Bungay, Suffolk
Filmset in Ehrhardt

*The publishers are grateful to the following Examination Boards for
permission to reproduce questions from examination papers used in
individual titles in the Passnotes series:*

*Associated Examination Board, University of Cambridge Local Examinations
Syndicate, Joint Matriculation Board, University of London School
Examinations Department, Oxford and Cambridge Schools Examination
Board, University of Oxford Delegacy of Local Examinations.*

*The Examination Boards accept no responsibility whatsoever for the
accuracy or method of working in any suggested answers given as models.*

Contents

To the student

This book is designed to help you with your O-level or C.S.E. English Literature examinations. It contains a synopsis of the plot, a glossary of the more unfamiliar words and phrases, and a commentary on some of the issues raised by the text. An account of the writer's life is also included for background.

Page references in parentheses refer to the Penguin Classics edition, edited by Martin Seymour-Smith.

When you use this book remember that it is no more than an aid to your study. It will help you find passages quickly and perhaps give you some ideas for essays. But remember: *This book is not a substitute for reading the text and it is your response and your knowledge that matter.* These are the things the examiners are looking for, and they are also the things that will give you the most pleasure. Show your knowledge and appreciation to the examiner, and show them clearly.

Introduction

BIOGRAPHICAL AND HISTORICAL NOTES

Thomas Hardy (1840–1928) completed *The Mayor of Casterbridge*
when he was forty-five years old. By that time he had a considerable
amount of writing experience, for this was his tenth novel.

Hardy had not begun his working life as a writer. Instead, he had
been trained as an architect. He had very sound connections in the
profession and received a sure grounding in its skills. It is interesting
to trace the many references to architectural styles within the novel
itself. He often yields to the temptation to provide minute attention
to architectural forms (pp. 96, 109, 129, 157, 211, etc.).

But, whilst training as an architect, Hardy was also fortunate to
have other influences which gave him a wider perspective. His love of
literature and his interest in writing began almost from the start of
his architectural career. The man to whom he was articled, John
Hicks of Dorchester, was a man of some education who also encouraged Hardy to be a scholar. There was another young man in
training with him at the time called Robert Boston and together they
mastered the classics, Latin and Greek. Hardy's life at this period,
where he fitted his classical studies into his private time, is not unlike
that of Elizabeth-Jane in the novel. Hardy's classical background
makes itself felt throughout his narrative, not just in such isolated
cases as this but in the rich vein of tragedy that is derived from the
Greek drama.

There is also a lot of colour in *The Mayor of Casterbridge* which
derives from Hardy's religious heritage. At one early period in his life
he seriously thought of taking Holy Orders. His close acquaintance

with the scriptures and the *Book of Common Prayer* is evident in many parts of the narrative. Not that Hardy, at the time of writing *The Mayor of Casterbridge*, was a religious man. He lived in an age of doubt: doubts about the validity of Christianity had been expressed by many leading scientific philosophers like John Stuart Mill, Charles Darwin, and others. Literature itself gave expression to these doubts, especially the poetry of the time.

Belief in God or in Christianity is not directly challenged in Hardy's *The Mayor of Casterbridge*, but there is a deep pessimism in the novel which reflects a world where people no longer believe that God is there to help them. No divine aid eases Henchard's suffering. Instead, the characters seem to be in the hands of a force which drives them despite any will of their own. And, in the case of Michael Henchard, it is a malignant power which destroys him completely.

Hardy's own philosophy was basically pessimistic despite his disclaimer that he was a pessimist 'only in so far as that character applies to a man who looks at the worst contingencies as well as the best in the human condition'. It was not his belief that the 'human condition' was being improved at all by the new materialistic advances that seemed to be sweeping religion and tradition aside. The sad sigh of Elizabeth-Jane, 'How things change!' (p. 240), might well be Hardy's own expression of concern.

His story begins in the first half of the nineteenth century. There the agricultural economy was ruled, like Henchard, by 'rule o' thumb'. The arrival of Donald Farfrae, an ambitious man destined for the New World, begins to change all that. The New World comes to Casterbridge. We see the beginnings of the railway (p. 339) as well as the spread of such machines as the seed-drill 'in the East and North of England' (p. 241). The move from the country to towns was increasing. The countryside was being deserted for towns like Casterbridge. This is illustrated in the despairing opening chapter of the novel where Henchard inquires about work in Weydon-Priors. A turnip-hoer tells him that 'Pulling down is more the nater of Weydin. There were five houses cleared away last year, and three this' (p. 71).

Inefficient business methods had to yield to a more professional approach. However, it is important to note that there is still a place for emotion in Hardy's view of things. Despite the 'entrepreneur', the businessman, in Farfrae, he can still extend concern and sympathy. Thus, there is that instance in chapter XIII where Farfrae prevents the separation of two lovers and, later, he is instrumental in setting Henchard up in business out of gratitude for his original generosity to him.

Emotion was a quality that Henchard possessed but which, unfortunately, never brought him satisfaction. It is not necessary to see Henchard as modelled on Hardy, but there are certain points where their experiences meet. Just as Henchard is unhappy in his marriage, so Hardy experienced considerable difficulties in his. He married a woman called Emma Gifford in 1874 soon after the publication, as a serial, of *Far From the Madding Crowd*. The omens were not altogether good: his father-in-law referred to him as a 'low born churl who had presumed to marry into my family'. Emma and Thomas found it hard to settle and they constantly moved house. It was not as if, like Henchard, Hardy had to move because of a search for work. His work was prolific and financially rewarding. It did not, however, always satisfy Emma. She did not encourage his writing. As she grew older she became more and more difficult and physically unattractive. Nevertheless Hardy did remain with her until she died. She was then seventy-two, as was Hardy. Just less than two years later, Hardy married a woman of thirty-five, Florence Dugdale. Again some comparison with Henchard and Lucetta is possible. Hardy had known Florence for ten years and we have no reason to believe that the relationship was merely platonic. One biographer says that Hardy was ready to 'fall immediately, if temporarily, in love with women glimpsed in the street, in railway carriages, on the tops of omnibuses, or indeed in any public place'. We remember that Henchard had his 'old flame' in Lucetta, and was quite prepared to marry her as soon as his wife was dead. Hardy seems to have had an equally unhappy marriage with Florence, and his biographers do not put all the blame on her by any means.

Wherever Hardy's heart may have been in relation to the various women he knew, it finally came to rest in the countryside he loved.

After his death in 1928 he was cremated, but his heart was first removed and was buried in the grave of his first wife, Emma, at Stinsford, near Dorchester. His ashes were buried in Westminster Abbey.

Synopsis of The Mayor of Casterbridge

Michael Henchard is a hay-trusser, unemployed and twenty-one years old. We are introduced to him as he, his wife and baby daughter trudge their way to Weydon-Priors. They are directed to a rural fair. Here, in the furmity tent, Henchard pays to have his drink laced with rum. He gets more and more drunk and, as he bemoans his fate, threatens to auction his wife Susan. A sailor called Newson eventually buys her for five guineas and Susan leaves with him, taking with her the infant Elizabeth-Jane. We learn later that the little 'family' emigrate to Canada. Susan believes herself truly bound to Newson. When a friend eventually persuades her this is not the case, Newson realizes their happiness is at an end, leaves and fakes the news of his death. Finally, nineteen years after the auction, Susan and her daughter return in search of Henchard. The Elizabeth-Jane we now see is fully grown. She is indeed Susan's daughter. However, she is not Henchard's. Her father is the sailor Newson (pp. 86–7).

In the nineteen years between the auction of his wife and her return, Henchard has become rich and powerful: the mayor of Casterbridge. This is the town he came to when he had finally abandoned the search for his wife and Elizabeth-Jane. He has sworn a great oath to renounce alcohol and this, coupled with his energies, has made him prosperous.

Having been directed to Casterbridge by the furmity-woman, Susan and Elizabeth-Jane find Henchard at the height of his power. They watch his mayoral dinner at the King's Arms. However, all is not well. We are told that Henchard is still a highly excitable character. We also learn that Henchard has sold the townsfolk 'growed wheat'. He can see no way round this problem or the people's anger until an anonymous Scot sends him a note informing him of a cure. At the close of the after-dinner speeches, Henchard makes his way to the Three Mariners, the pub where Farfrae, the young Scot, has gone. There, also, Susan and Elizabeth-Jane are staying.

Elizabeth-Jane helps pay her way by serving at the pub. She waits on Farfrae, to whom she is attracted (p. 113). Meanwhile, her mother has heard the conversation between Henchard and Farfrae through the thin walls. Having at first flinched from her husband's magnificence she is now encouraged to send Elizabeth-Jane to him with a message ambiguously informing him of their presence.

Henchard, meanwhile, has earnestly besought Farfrae to stay in Casterbridge. The young man had previously been on his way to America. Farfrae has solved Henchard's problem with the wheat and revealed himself as an efficient, modern, technological farmer. Finally, Henchard's offers win him over. He will become Henchard's manager instead of Joshua Jopp to whom Henchard had half promised the job.

Henchard meets Elizabeth-Jane, winces to hear her call Newson father and sends her back to her mother with five guineas and instructions to meet him in 'the Ring', a sinister Roman ruin outside Casterbridge and by repute a place unfavourable to lovers. Here Henchard, revealing a stern sense of duty, tells that he is prepared to set Susan up in a cottage, pay court to her until he can 'remarry' her and, above all, try to keep knowledge of the past from Elizabeth-Jane (pp. 143–4). That Susan does not reveal at this point that Elizabeth-Jane is Newson's daughter rather than Henchard's shows how manipulating this apparently harmless woman can be.

Henchard returns from his bizarre meeting and resolves to open his heart to his new friend Farfrae. The lonely, impulsive man reveals the story of the wife auction, the drama of his wife's return and, something we did not know until this point, the fact that he has promised to marry Lucetta, his Jersey mistress of some long standing. Both Henchard and Farfrae realize that Henchard's overriding duty is to his first wife and 'child'. His past has caught up with him.

Henchard grimly courts Susan and eventually 'remarries' her. She moves into Henchard's house with her daughter, who raises Henchard's slight suspicions when he notices that the colour of her hair is not his. However, he takes neither this nor the fact that Susan persuades Elizabeth-Jane against adopting Henchard's surname any further. Having dealt with these problems, Susan continues to further her daughter's career by faking notes to engineer a meeting between Farfrae and Elizabeth-Jane. Susan wants her daughter to marry Henchard's efficient young manager (p. 163).

The first sign of a rift between Henchard and Farfrae is observed by Elizabeth-Jane. Henchard tries to humiliate Abel Whittle, one of his workmen, after repeated lateness. Farfrae threatens to resign at this. Henchard becomes suspicious of Farfrae's appeal to the ordinary people and reacts as violently but unfavourably to him as he had been generous when he first took him in. A cold politeness settles between the two men, a state of affairs worsened when Farfrae's celebration of a 'national event' attracts all the people away from Henchard's despite Farfrae's charging admission. Henchard goes to Farfrae's celebration, hears the townsfolk talk about Farfrae's ascendency, and becomes violently jealous. He hastily hints to Farfrae that he is going to dismiss him and Farfrae takes him at his word (pp. 178–9).

Farfrae leaves Henchard despite his growing attraction for Elizabeth-Jane. He sets up his own business, making the competition between himself and his sometime friend as decent as possible. Henchard, furious, forbids Elizabeth-Jane to see the young man. Farfrae, whose feelings do not run deep, agrees to this. However, we are now to see the rise of the modern, mechanized Farfrae and the fall of the old-fashioned, impulsive Henchard.

As Susan dies we are told of the arrival in Casterbridge of Lucetta. We will soon learn that she has inherited money from an aunt, taken her surname and plans to live in Casterbridge. She is no longer financially dependent on Henchard. She asks for the return of her love letters. As Henchard makes his way to see her, the dying Susan informs Elizabeth-Jane that it was she who engineered the meeting between Farfrae and the girl. She also writes a letter to Henchard informing him that Elizabeth-Jane is Newson's daughter. She requests that the letter should not be opened until Elizabeth-Jane's wedding day but fails to seal the letter properly. Susan Henchard then dies.

Three weeks after her death Henchard begs Elizabeth-Jane to take his name, telling her she is his daughter and offering to prove she is so with certain papers. When Henchard goes to search for these he finds Susan's letter. He opens the inadequate seal and discovers Susan's confession that Elizabeth-Jane is her daughter by Newson. Henchard is appalled but vows to make Elizabeth-Jane continue to think herself his own daughter. Elizabeth-Jane joyfully accepts this role, accepts Henchard as her true father, but her likeness to Newson is perfectly clear to Henchard who becomes increasingly cold to her.

When Elizabeth-Jane, mortified by Henchard's incomprehensible reaction to her, one day goes to visit her mother's grave, she meets with a fine lady who asks Elizabeth-Jane to be her companion. Elizabeth-Jane is delighted to escape from her father and to be given the chance to learn how to be the lady Henchard has reviled her for not being. Happiness seems hers. Elizabeth-Jane does not realize that the fine lady is none other than Lucetta, Henchard's mistress, come now to claim him as her husband.

Elizabeth-Jane moves to Lucetta's house at High-Place Hall, telling her father where she is going only as she is on the point of departure. Henchard now knows that Lucetta has moved to Casterbridge and when he discovers that his 'daughter' is to be Lucetta's companion he is horrified (p. 217).

Lucetta, of course, has taken on Elizabeth-Jane so that Henchard may have a reason for visiting her, a reason that will not arouse suspicion. Her plan seems foiled when Elizabeth-Jane tells Lucetta that she and her father have quarrelled so badly that he will never visit her. Lucetta is deeply upset. She contrives that Elizabeth-Jane leave the house and writes to Henchard to tell him she is alone. She rises excitedly at the sound of a man's step but is not faced with Henchard. The man she sees is Farfrae who has been allowed to resume his courtship of Elizabeth-Jane. Lucetta is immediately interested in the young man (p. 229).

Farfrae and Lucetta are suddenly and deeply attracted to each other. Henchard is now nothing to Lucetta. She refuses to see him and will keep Elizabeth-Jane on only to drive Henchard away.

Both Lucetta and Elizabeth-Jane watch the market place in order to glimpse Farfrae. One day they see him with a new seed drill, an implement of the new technology. Elizabeth-Jane watches the growing relationship between Farfrae and Lucetta which she does not fully understand. Lucetta is increasingly cold towards Henchard who begins to suspect an affair between his sometime friend and mistress. Elizabeth-Jane, watching all three of them, finds the situation ridiculous.

Henchard vows to defeat Farfrae in business and hires Jopp to help him. This is the man whom he was going to hire as manager before Farfrae arrived. Risking all on a change in the weather, Henchard buys wheat at high prices, hoping that they will rise even further. His hopes are supported by the advice of a weather-prophet. However, the weather is excellent, prices fall and Farfrae buys in at a very cheap rate. Only then does the weather change. Farfrae prospers and Henchard is financially ruined (p. 261).

Henchard is now ruined both socially and in his love life. His suspicions of an affair between Farfrae and Lucetta are confirmed and he blackmails Lucetta into a promise of marriage. The following day he acts as the local magistrate. The accused is none other than the furmity-woman, who exposes Henchard's past. Henchard manfully accepts that he is in no position to be the woman's judge and, so great is the ensuing scandal, that Lucetta declares that she must flee Casterbridge. She does so not simply to avoid Henchard and her forced promise of marriage, but to wed Farfrae and so escape her financially-and socially-ruined former lover. Lucetta returns, secretly wed. Henchard saves her from a savage attack by a bull. Lucetta asks how she may thank him, but when Henchard asks her to tell his creditors he is about to wed this rich woman, Lucetta has to reveal her marriage to Farfrae. Henchard is horrified. To sudden financial and social ruin is added the ruin of his love life. His complete destruction is about to come about.

Farfrae moves into High-Place Hall with Lucetta. Elizabeth-Jane is mortified and, when she hears of Lucetta's previous relationship with Henchard, the man she still believes to be her father, she vows to leave Lucetta and live on her own.

Henchard's bankruptcy is confirmed. In his defeat he acts with great dignity but is forced to watch Farfrae buy up his businesses and run them on more efficient, modern lines. Farfrae offers to take Henchard into his old house, which he has now bought, but Henchard refuses. He is nursed through an illness by Elizabeth-Jane but, when better, is obliged to seek work under Farfrae in his old business. The humiliation is great and, the time of his vow of abstinence now being up, Henchard begins to drink again (p. 303). He begins also to taunt Farfrae and Lucetta. Elizabeth-Jane wonders if he might even be planning to murder them. She goes to Farfrae who offers to set Henchard up in a little business. He has no ill feelings towards his former rival but is unable to go through with his offer when he learns of Elizabeth-Jane's suspicions.

Farfrae becomes mayor of Casterbridge. Lucetta, in some distress, asks Henchard for the return of her love letters which are in a wall safe in Henchard's old house. He returns there and reads the letters to Farfrae, the new owner of the house. Henchard is clearly burning for revenge. We expect him to reveal to Farfrae that the woman concerned in the letters is none other than Lucetta, now Farfrae's wife. However, Henchard's feelings are too great, too generous, to allow him to make such an exposure. He cannot even bring himself to humiliate Lucetta when they are alone. In defeat, Henchard grows in moral stature.

The rustics, nonetheless, are determined to humiliate both Farfrae and Lucetta. They come to learn of the love letters and their contents and plan a 'skimmington-ride', a public exhibition of what they see as Lucetta's adultery (p. 334).

While this is being planned, a royal visit is also due to Casterbridge. It will be Farfrae and Lucetta's social triumph and Henchard is determined to wreck it. Pathetically, he staggers out to pay his homage to the 'Royal Personage' but is removed by Farfrae.

The rustics, determined to humble Lucetta, prepare the skimmington while Henchard, determined to humble Farfrae, challenges him to a fight. He gets the young man at his mercy but then, bitterly ashamed of himself, lets him go (p. 348).

The organizers of the skimmington send Farfrae on a wild goose chase but their effect on the pregnant Lucetta is fatal. Henchard learns of this, sets out after Farfrae and catches up with him, but Farfrae refuses to believe Henchard's news of his wife's state. He believes Henchard still wishes to kill him. Henchard's heroic effort has been in vain and he returns to Jopp's house only to hear of the arrival of Newson. Henchard lies to the sailor. He tells him Elizabeth-Jane is dead and Newson appears to believe him (p. 367).

Henchard shows his growing human sympathy in defeat. Not only does he show magnanimity to Farfrae and Lucetta, he also begins to appreciate Elizabeth-Jane's full worth. As a result, troubled by his lies over her true father, he contemplates suicide. He is saved from this, but there are further humiliations he must endure. He accepts the Council's gift of the seed-shop and he runs the place well. However, he comes to realize that his rival is now courting Elizabeth-Jane, the only human contact left to him. He is terrified he will be rejected and left alone. He becomes increasingly morbid, and when Elizabeth-Jane receives an anonymous letter from, as Henchard rightly supposes, Newson, he resolves to free the girl. Rather than be revealed by Newson, Henchard dresses as a hay-trusser and, broken and defeated, goes out in search of work as he did at the start of the novel (p. 388). The wheel has turned full circle. Newson comes to claim Elizabeth-Jane as his own daughter and encourages her wedding with Farfrae. Henchard, unable to leave the environs of Casterbridge, determines to see his 'daughter's' happiness and resolves to visit the town on her wedding day. He is allowed to glimpse a happiness in which he has no part, indeed from which he is an exile. Elizabeth-Jane is hard to him because of his lies about her father. Henchard slips away from the wedding celebrations to die in the hovel of Abel Whittle, the man who had exposed Henchard's rift with Farfrae, the first sign of Henchard's tragedy. Henchard's will reveals his bitterness, his self-hatred. He has lost wife, daughter, mistress, friend and money. All he cared for and all he made has been taken from him. He can leave the world nothing but his wish to be forgotten. It is this will Farfrae and Elizabeth-Jane discover half an hour after his lonely death. Henchard's final tragic agony is over. His rival has married the one surviving woman he loved, the girl he thought his daughter. It is with her that the novel closes. She is a modest, stoical, accepting woman who, exposed to tragedy and the ironies of fate, realizes that life is fundamentally painful and that happiness is but 'the occasional episode in a general drama of pain'.

An Account of the Plot

Hardy's novel opens with great visual impact. It is like a film. We see a young man and a woman with a child trudging through the countryside. We do not know who they are and we can only guess at their relationship. Nonetheless, by carefully accumulating details, Hardy tells us a great deal about his anonymous characters. We learn through our eyes that these are country people. The man carries the tools of his trade with him. The couple have come a long way and are dusty from their journey. The impression of rural people at one with the countryside will be important to the novel as will the mood of pessimism Hardy so powerfully conveys. It is clear from the start that the couple are not happy with each other. Whatever love there may have been between them has died. The man shows 'a dogged and cynical indifference'. He is pretending to read in order not to talk to the woman. She, for her part, seems to welcome his indifference. She is not beautiful, except when she looks down at the child; but as he describes her, Hardy makes a major theme of his novel clear: the idea that man is ruled by Time and Chance and that these forces are not kindly disposed to him (p. 70). Life does not bring pleasure, we cannot expect 'fair play' and, as Hardy writes at the close of the novel, happiness is only an 'occasional episode in a general drama of pain'.

This tragic mood is the essence of the book. The characters in *The Mayor of Casterbridge* struggle against Fate, strive after contentment, but are broken down by Time, Chance and Fate. Even the landscape through which this couple are walking reflects the feeling of defeat. It is ugly and dull. The leaves are 'doomed', dying. When the couple meet a labourer, it becomes clear not only that life is hard but that even earning a living is difficult. There is no work about. Poverty is added to the 'general drama of pain'.

Having established this mood, Hardy brings his couple to the fair and so launches on one of the most famous and bizzare chapters in English literature. The couple make their way to the furmity tent. The man slyly pays to have his furmity laced with rum and as he gets more and more drunk, he bemoans his poverty and unhappy marriage. Outside we hear the end of a horse auction. Ideas merge in the drunk man's mind and he thinks of selling his wife off to the highest bidder, like the horses outside. The comparison is tellingly ironic and the rustics in the furmity tent are shocked. However, this is not the first time such a sale has been threatened, as the woman comments (p. 76). Indeed, wife auctions such as this were not wholly unknown in real life. But what this one brings out is the brutality, the cruelty and impulsiveness of Henchard. When drunk, he is a pathetic creature.

Susan, of course, finds a buyer. The sailor Newson arrives and pays five guineas for her. What had seemed almost a joke now becomes a matter of deadly earnest. Susan asserts that if her husband takes Newson's money she will leave him. The drunk husband shouts out that he is far from playing. He picks up the coins, folds the banknotes and pockets them 'with an air of finality'. Susan makes her decision too. She flings down her wedding ring and walks out with the sailor and her child.

Henchard struggles to the entrance of the tent. Outside, he glimpses the vast, indifferent panorama of nature. Ironically, the horses are tender to each other, far more tender than this man to his woman. The appalled rustics slowly go home; Henchard, in a drunken stupor, slumps over the table.

It is all highly dramatic, even sensational. The reader is both amazed and appalled. But what has Hardy done in addition to exciting us? He has set into action the whole course of his novel. We have seen that he views the world as tragic and painful. We have seen the failure of love. We have seen a cruel, drunk, impulsive man free himself from the burden of an unloved wife and child. Henchard has tried to make himself a free man. He has lashed out against constraints. Perhaps he is at liberty to start a new life. But this cannot be. When Henchard has abandoned his remorseful searching after his wife and child and sworn his great oath to abjure alcohol he will indeed start a new existence. He will become a rich man, a successful and ambitious careerist, the mayor of Casterbridge. We have seen he is brutal and impulsive; we will come to see his heroic energy and drive. However, it is the central irony of the book that this passionate and in many ways worthy man will be destroyed by what he did to set himself free. When Susan and Elizabeth-Jane return, these innocent and rather naïve women will bring about the destruction of Henchard. And it is his own fault. The drunkard slumped over the table will wake and rouse himself. He will achieve great things, but he will be destroyed by his past actions. The destruction of this man is the subject of the novel. Because the process of Henchard's destruction raises feelings of pity and awe, the novel may truly be called a tragedy.

CHAPTER II, *pp. 82–5*

Henchard wakes from his drunken sleep and discovers his wife's wedding ring on the floor of the furmity tent. He feels Newson's banknotes in his pocket and begins to realize the truth of his plight. Henchard pieces together the events of the previous evening, gathers up his belongings, and makes his troubled way from the still sleeping fair.

After walking for a mile, Henchard stops to think. He wonders if he gave any clue to his identity while he was drunk. He realizes too that he must try to find his wife, whom he blames for her 'idiotic simplicity' and her 'meekness' that have done him so much harm (p. 84). These two characteristics of Susan will be crucial to Henchard's later downfall. He also resolves to swear a great oath to renounce drink for twenty-one years. He finds a church, enters it, and makes his mighty and solemn vow. Hardy calls this 'fetishistic', but Henchard has at least 'made a start in a new direction'.

For some months Henchard searches for his wife and child. Ironically, he even spends the money he had earned from their sale in the search. However, he is unsuccessful. He is too 'shy' to follow the search through fully and eventually he gives up, journeying south-west until he reaches Casterbridge. Apparently he is now a free man able to start a new life. The past that had so tied down the man has disappeared. We shall not see Henchard for another nineteen years. During this time he will have realized his potential. He will have become rich and powerful: the mayor of Casterbridge.

CHAPTER III, *pp. 86–90*

We are introduced to Susan and Elizabeth-Jane making their way through the countryside to Weydon-Priors. Nature, the landscape, is timeless and unchanging. Time, however, has aged and hardened Susan's face and matured Elizabeth-Jane to a 'well-formed young woman'. It is clear from her looks that she is her mother's daughter. That she is not Henchard's will only be revealed later and in tragic circumstances.

The two women make their way to the fair which is a much poorer business than before, agricultural advances having largely replaced its purpose. This will be an important theme in the novel.

They have come to the fair, as Susan explains, to look for their 'relation', for Henchard. Susan refuses to tell her daughter precisely what relation the man is to her and says he may even be dead. Newson, it appears, is certainly dead. That he is not dead, as we shall later discover, is yet a further tragic irony.

The women make their way to the dilapidated furmity stand where Susan questions the impoverished furmity seller about the wife auction. The old woman cannot recall it. It was not a 'big' enough thing (p. 89). She will, of course, recall the scene vividly enough when she is on trial before Henchard (p. 274) but now she has to strain to remember how the man who sold his wife came back to inform her that he is living in Casterbridge. Thither, the following morning, the two women make their way. The impression of the mild Susan's remorseless search is a strong one. We begin to feel that Henchard is truly doomed.

CHAPTER IV, *pp. 91–8*

These so seemingly ineffectual instruments of vengeance make their way to Casterbridge with some financial difficulty (p. 94). Hardy uses their journey as an opportunity briefly to relate something of what has happened to Susan, Elizabeth-Jane and Newson in the interim.

Susan has not told her daughter the whole truth for fear of losing her affection, while her 'idiotic simplicity' has made her think she is truly Newson's wife. The little 'family' worked hard in Canada and were fairly happy until a friend of Susan's told her the truth about her 'marriage'. Newson realizes that his happiness is at an end. He leaves home and the 'vague news' is received of his loss at sea. Elizabeth-Jane grows up and her mother is concerned about their poverty and her daughter's lack of opportunity. She determines to 'advance' her now she is free of Newson (p. 93). She resolves to set out in search of her true husband. However, she decides not to tell Elizabeth-Jane the whole story but to let matters sort themselves out when Henchard is located. The plot of the novel concerns the tragic unfolding of the truth.

The women arrive at Casterbridge (p. 94) and Elizabeth-Jane declares it rather old-fashioned. They hear Henchard's name mentioned by some locals and they make their way to the centre of the town where they can hear a brass band playing. The wholly agricultural nature of Casterbridge is described (p. 96). We then learn (p. 97) that the local corn-factor has been selling 'growed wheat' and that the poor people are suffering from bad bread as a result. We sense there is ill feeling in Casterbridge.

CHAPTER V, *pp. 99–105*

The women follow the music of the band and come to the centre of the town and the front of the King's Arms. This is the chief hotel in Casterbridge and a celebration is in progress there. The women make inquiries and discover that this is the feast of the corn-factor, the mayor, of Michael Henchard himself. The poor people stand outside to watch his triumph and, by describing the hotel in such a way that the people are physically below the window of the banqueting chamber, Hardy at once emphasizes the height to which Henchard has risen and the depth to which he must return. This is a fine example of Hardy's art.

Susan stares at her husband. She sees a man coarse and swarthy with flashing black eyes (p. 100). The impression of a domineering and emotional man is built up through the chapter. Great though Henchard has become, the impulsiveness of his character is still there. It will help destroy him. It is clear also (p. 101) that Henchard has kept to his vow of abstinence from alcohol which has another two years to run. The rustics comment on this and, as always, their words are full of foreboding. Elizabeth-Jane is impressed by Henchard's magnificence but her mother flinches from it.

The rustics also comment on Henchard's rise to a position of wealth. They are impressed by this self-made man but they are also angered by the poor quality of the bread made from his corn. Their protests at this become louder (p. 104). Henchard hears. He tries to excuse himself and says he will welcome any suggestion as to what can be done. He himself is sure that nothing can improve matters. Hardy comments significantly on his reaction to criticism, however: 'Henchard's face darkened. There was a temper under the thin bland surface – the temper which, artificially intensified, had banished a wife nearly a score of years before.' We have seen Henchard in triumph; we have seen also that his fundamental nature has not changed. We have glimpsed what will lead to his downfall: his past, his old-fashioned agricultural methods, his volatile character.

CHAPTER VI, *pp. 106–10*

We are introduced to a slightly-built, bright-eyed stranger whose ear has been caught by Henchard's fatalistic belief that nothing can be done to the 'growed wheat'. The unnamed man with a Scottish accent writes a note and has it passed to Henchard. This is the first of many notes that will precipitate Henchard's downfall. The unnamed man then makes his way to the Three Mariners, a place far less expensive than the King's Arms, leaving Henchard to brood in a 'fitful intense' way on his note while the rest of his party drink themselves into high spirits (p. 107).

Susan and Elizabeth-Jane also make their way to the Three Mariners. Just as they leave, Henchard comes out, makes inquiries about who sent him the note and, learning where the man is, makes his way to the Three Mariners as well. Thus Hardy very neatly gets all his major characters under one roof.

Hardy's description of the Three Mariners and its customers (p. 109) makes it clear that the pub belongs to a lower social order than that with which the mayor is familiar. Henchard himself is now walking unwittingly to his fate, the fall that will result in the loss of all his prestige. For the moment, however, he is obsessed with meeting the writer of the note and enters the pub, 'lowering the dignity of his presence as much as possible by buttoning the brown holland coat over his shirt front, and in other ways toning himself down to his ordinary everyday appearance'.

CHAPTER VII, *pp. 111–18*

The women have been shown a room which they fear is too expensive for them. They are concerned to be 'respectable', but as Susan feels they cannot appeal to Henchard for money, Elizabeth-Jane realizes she must offer her services to the management to help defray costs (p. 112). Almost at once she is asked to service the Scotsman with his supper. She finds him in a room close to her own and is immediately attracted to him (p. 113).

The landlady allows Elizabeth-Jane to take her own supper. She goes to her room where she finds her mother listening in amazement to the conversation next door. Their room is divided from the Scotsman's by only the thinnest of partitions and the voice she can hear is none other than Henchard's.

Henchard believes the man to have come to answer to his advertisement for a manager. The young Scot tells him this is not the case. He introduces himself as Donald Farfrae and tells Henchard he is off to 'the great wheat-growing districts of America'. Henchard is disappointed, but on questioning Farfrae about the 'growed-wheat' is shown a device by which it can be restored. Farfrae is at once established as a modern, technological farmer. Henchard pays tribute to this and also expresses his own weaknesses which will contribute to his financial ruin when he declares: 'unluckily I am bad at science, Farfrae; bad at figures – a rule o' thumb sort of man'. This contrast between the old and the new approaches to agriculture will be of the utmost importance in the novel.

Henchard realizes Farfrae's worth and does his utmost to persuade the young Scot to stay. For the moment he appears unsuccessful. For the reader, the cruel irony lies in Henchard's pleading with the man who is to help towards his destruction to stay with him rather than 'see the warruld'.

CHAPTER VIII, *pp. 119–25*

Farfrae appears sociable. He rings for Elizabeth-Jane to clear his supper things and then joins the company below whom he entertains with Scottish folk-songs (p. 120). All are moved by these. Even the scientific Farfrae reveals the other side of his hardheaded nature. The rustics comment that Farfrae's songs reveal a purer and more poetic world than the Casterbridge which, significantly, they characterize as 'a old, hoary place o' wickedness'. As the drinks and songs go round the rustics begin to invest Farfrae with 'a golden haze' (p. 122). This is the first indication of the great popularity and power that will be wished onto him, to Henchard's detriment.

Farfrae is insistent that he is leaving for America (p. 124). This causes disappointment, not least to Elizabeth-Jane who has been observing him closely. They pass each other and it is clear that Farfrae finds her fairly attractive. Susan, however, is worried in case Henchard find out that she has acted as a serving-maid. She refers to Henchard as 'he'. Elizabeth-Jane misunderstands her and believes she is referring to Farfrae, and she rather charmingly shows in what affection she holds the Scot.

The chapter ends with the lonely, impulsive Henchard who has also been deeply struck by Farfrae. Had he stayed Henchard would have given him a third of his business.

CHAPTER IX, *pp. 126–34*

As Elizabeth-Jane looks at rural Casterbridge she glimpses Henchard. He, in turn, sees Farfrae and offers to walk with him to his coach. We see Elizabeth-Jane here as an unseen observer. This will frequently be the case in the novel. Both Henchard and Elizabeth-Jane are sorry to be losing Farfrae.

Susan, meanwhile, has been encouraged to contact Henchard by observing his warmth towards Farfrae, his obvious wealth (which she desires for her daughter's sake) and her hearing Henchard described as a lonely widower, ashamed of his past. She decides to send Elizabeth-Jane with an ambiguous message (p. 128). Her irresolution is clear.

Elizabeth-Jane picks her way through crowded Casterbridge. The description gives at once the impression of a busy agricultural town and, on another level, the complex entanglements Elizabeth-Jane is about to face. She eventually finds her goal and enters to see not Henchard but Farfrae. We are told why. Henchard has taken so warmly to Farfrae, pressed him so hard and offered him so much, that Farfrae realizes he must accept. He sees this as Providence, Fate (p. 133), and so becomes Henchard's man. This is the first unconscious step to replacing him.

Henchard, again described as a 'man of strong impulses', has got what he wants. The bitter irony is that he has taken in the man who will destroy him. He has even asked him to live in his house (p. 134). For the moment Henchard's heart is warmed. Farfrae sees that Fate has led him to complete a rich deal for himself.

CHAPTER X, *pp. 135–9*

Dramatic irony and, with it, the means of Henchard's destruction gather momentum. Chapter X opens with the arrival of Joshua Jopp just as Henchard ushers Elizabeth-Jane into his office. Joshua Jopp is the man who has answered Henchard's advertisement for a manager. Although, as Jopp says, Henchard has as good as engaged him, he now turns him away. Jopp is late. A better man has been found.

The interview between Henchard and Elizabeth-Jane is beautifully understated, particularly by Henchard who is deeply gratified that Susan has told neither this girl nor the world of what had happened at the fair. He takes the girl through to his house, questions her about Newson and, assuming her to be his daughter, winces to hear her call Newson father. Carefully, he extracts from Elizabeth-Jane what she knows of her family history (p. 137). He then writes a note to Susan and sends five pounds with it. As an afterthought he adds five shillings. He has sent five guineas, the sum he sold Susan for. The irony is exact.

Henchard, not unnaturally, is overwhelmed by these events, but, for the moment, he can lightly comment: 'It never rains but it pours!' He has, however, arranged to meet his wife in secrecy that evening. The atmosphere of conspiracy and secrecy which is so important to the novel deepens.

CHAPTER XI, *pp. 140–45*

The place Henchard has chosen for the meeting is 'the Ring at Casterbridge', a sinister Roman remain, vast, lonely and associated with death. Above all, it is not a place for happy lovers (p. 141). In the previous chapter, Hardy had set up his tragic ironies; now he indulges his taste for the sensational and macabre to suggest what Henchard's renewed relation with Susan will entail: secrecy, suffering and death. He suggests the timelessness of pain. Henchard's reason for choosing this place is secrecy. He is ashamed but he is also worried by what might happen.

In their interview Susan reveals that she thought herself truly bound to Newson. There is certainly no joy in Henchard's heart. He sees the necessity of their living together and preserving the truth from Elizabeth-Jane, whom he believes to be his daughter. Susan does not correct him about this. She has her reasons.

Henchard has decided that the best plan is for Susan to take a cottage, live as the widowed Mrs Newson and be 'courted' by Henchard until it is reasonable for them to 'marry'. Susan reveals her entire dependence on Henchard and the fact that she is acting solely for Elizabeth-Jane's benefit. She has, and this the worldly Henchard does not suspect, a deep-seated and simple cunning. For all her naïvety, Susan Henchard is a dangerous woman.

She agrees to Henchard's plan, but it is not made clear if she forgives him for the past (p. 145). Henchard, for his part, asks to be judged by his 'future works'.

CHAPTER XII, *pp. 146–51*

The future, however, will be complicated by past events of which even the reader is, at the moment, unaware.

Henchard returns home after his encounter to find Farfrae doing the account books. The contrast makes for excellent characterization. Henchard has returned from a scene of high melodrama, Farfrae is seen as industrious, methodical, analytic. Henchard, as Hardy describes him, 'was mentally and physically unfit for grubbing subtleties from sordid paper'. Unfortunately, it is precisely such labour that preserves fortunes.

Henchard refuses to let Farfrae work on. He is lonely and troubled. He has no one else to talk to and so he opens his heart to Farfrae (p. 147). He tells him the story of Susan and Elizabeth-Jane but adds what the reader has not been told: the story of his affair with Lucetta, his Jersey mistress.

He rightly declares that it was impossible for him to live wholly without a woman. He is subject to loneliness 'and the blackness of hell'. These are depths of emotion Farfrae does not experience.

Lucetta was fairly well bred. She had nursed Henchard through an illness. They fell in love but she, careless as she was, involved herself in a scandal by being indiscreet. She suffered for this and wrote to Henchard to tell him so. These letters, like all the others in the book, will be of significance. Eventually it transpires that Henchard has proposed to her. The bitter irony is that he cannot marry her as his true wife has now come back to him. Henchard wants to treat both women well (p. 150) but he is in a dreadful dilemma. To Farfrae the issue is simple: Henchard must return to Susan. Henchard agrees, but feels he must pay Lucetta off. He asks Farfrae to help him draft a letter to this effect. Farfrae agrees to do so. He is then told of Elizabeth-Jane. Henchard believes she is his own daughter. Elizabeth-Jane thinks she is Newson's daughter. That the latter is the true position only Susan knows for certain. The springs of tragedy are tightly wound.

The chapter ends with Henchard wondering if he can rid himself of what seems his lightest encumbrance – Lucetta – as easily as he has planned to. Of course, he cannot.

CHAPTER XIII, *pp. 152–6*

Henchard is invited to tea in the cottage he has obtained for Susan and Elizabeth-Jane. Hardy comments (beginning of the chapter):

> The visit was repeated again and again with business-like determination by the Mayor, who seemed to have schooled himself into a course of strict mechanical rightness towards this woman of prior claim, at any expense to the later one and to his own sentiments.

Such behaviour is false to Henchard's true nature and when Henchard suggests that he and Susan 'name the happy day' we detect a note of bitter irony. Susan falters but is encouraged by Henchard (p. 153) and their affair becomes a matter for local gossip. The people cannot fully understand it and assume it is some matter of family convenience, for they know the two are related in some way. Of course, they do not know how closely. The local schoolboys nickname Susan 'The Ghost'. This again is ironic for Susan is indeed a spectre from Henchard's past come to haunt him.

Henchard himself proceeds in an unflinching, conscientious way (p. 153). There is no love in what he does, only three resolves: to make amends to Susan, to provide for the girl he thinks is his daughter and to punish himself.

The wedding takes place (p. 154). Farfrae, who knows a great deal about the situation, is unmoved by the drama of it. Only the ignorant rustics joke amongst themselves about their own chances of such strange affairs and marriages.

CHAPTER XIV, *pp. 157–65*

Susan moves into Henchard's house. He is as kind to her as he can be but she makes little impression. Elizabeth-Jane, on the other hand, begins to flourish as an attractive woman, fresh, serious and steady. She is too aware of how lucky she is to tempt Providence with expensive clothes and other outward signs of her new good fortune. However, she is attractive and is recognized as such by Henchard (p. 159). He looks at her more closely and, remembering how his wife had said when Elizabeth-Jane was a baby that her hair would be black, wonders why it is a lightish brown. Of course, this is a sign that Elizabeth-Jane is not who her mother has told him she is, not the black-haired Henchard's child at all. Susan manages to disguise her embarrassment at Henchard's question but he, deepening the irony of which he is wholly unaware, asks that Elizabeth-Jane change her surname to his. The girl agrees, but Susan (the only one of the three to know the whole truth) is flustered and later asks her daughter if she does not think she is being disrespectful to Newson in wanting to change her surname. Elizabeth-Jane agrees to discuss the matter with Henchard and eventually the subject is dropped.

Meanwhile, Henchard's business thrives under Farfrae's management. Elizabeth-Jane, who so frequently acts as an unseen observer in the novel, discerns 'Henchard's tigerish affection for the younger man'. She is, however, puzzled and a little hurt by the curiosity with which Farfrae observes her mother. She would much prefer for him to look at her. She is quite unaware, of course, of what Farfrae knows. We are given the impression of a naïve, innocent, but loving girl caught in circumstances of which she is unaware.

Susan, however, is well aware that her daughter's situation needs further advancing. Just as Elizabeth-Jane moves silently and passively through the novel, observing many things and often acting as Hardy's eyes, so Susan, the quiet, dull and seemingly ineffectual woman, silently works to advance Hardy's plot. She writes two notes: one for Farfrae and one for Elizabeth-Jane. In this way she hopes to bring the two young people together. It is an act she confesses to only on her deathbed.

The young people do indeed meet and are embarrassed and confused. Farfrae himself certainly does not take immediate advantage of the situation. Indeed, he is rather annoyed that his time is being wasted (p. 164). However, Elizabeth-Jane's mention of his singing raises some emotion in him and, as he sees the wheat chaff on Elizabeth-Jane's dress, his voice takes on 'tones of extreme delicacy'. Elizabeth-Jane neither assents nor demurs as he blows them off, but his breath on her neck clearly excites her and seems to rouse Farfrae sufficiently for him to become reluctant to get back to business. There is an eroticism here that would be wholly charming if we could avoid the thought that such happiness has been far too easily come by and cannot last.

CHAPTER XV, *pp. 166–72*

At first, Farfrae alone is attracted by Elizabeth-Jane's growing beauty, but she learns to dress herself to advantage and her new-found sexuality begins to make her 'distinctively feminine' (p. 167). However, Elizabeth-Jane is troubled by this discovery and begins to hanker after learning and accomplishments rather than mere physical beauty.

One day, as she looks at Henchard and Farfrae, she sees the start of those incidents that are to break their friendship. Hardy compares this to the moment a seed takes root. It is an ironic metaphor. Elizabeth-Jane sees Henchard upbraid Abel Whittle for being late: Whittle is warned that he is not to be late again. Henchard is adamant, despite Whittle's pathetic excuses. The following day Whittle is indeed late once more. Henchard goes to his cottage and drives the man to work without his 'breeches'. Farfrae objects to this, orders the man home to dress and, when questioned by Henchard, declares that either Whittle is allowed to dress or he will walk out. The scene is farcical. Farfrae accuses Henchard of being a tyrant; Henchard accuses Farfrae of taking advantage of him because he knows of his secret life. The Scot replies that he has forgotten all about it, but it is clear that Henchard's resentment of Farfrae is both deep and sudden, typical of his impulsive nature. The request by a local family that Farfrae rather than Henchard judge the value of their haystack only adds to Henchard's increasing feeling of inferiority. Farfrae has unintentionally won the ordinary people to his side. He seems to them both more humane and wiser. Eventually, Henchard makes a sort of peace with Farfrae, who has not really understood the nature of his employer's resentment, but Hardy comments that Henchard now thinks of Farfrae with 'a dim dread' and regrets that he had told him the story of his secret life. Again, Henchard, the man of impulse, has been made insecure by the violence and alternating nature of his feelings.

CHAPTER XVI, *pp. 173–9*

Henchard becomes more reserved and formal in his dealings with Farfrae now but matters are brought to a new head when Farfrae proposes a celebration for a 'national event' (p. 173). Henchard, although he is mayor, has organized nothing so far but now decides to set something up at his own expense. He discovers that Farfrae has decided to charge admission to his gathering and Henchard is yet more dismissive when he sees Farfrae's seemingly unattractive attempt at a marquee (p. 175). Henchard's entertainment is set out in the open air.

The day for the celebration arrives but it pours with rain. No one comes to enjoy Henchard's entertainment and he is told that all the locals are with Farfrae. Henchard goes to investigate and finds everyone enjoying themselves enormously. They are dancing. Farfrae is dressed in Highland costume. Elizabeth-Jane clearly enjoys the whole thing but Henchard, haunting the shadows, hears himself and his efforts criticized. The rise of Farfrae in the people's affection is becoming clearer. The men remain polite to each other but Henchard 'planted on Donald an antagonistic glare that had begun as a smile'. The final blow to Henchard's pride comes from the jocular Mr Tubber (p. 178). Henchard gloomily hints that Farfrae will not be working for him much longer. Farfrae takes the hint. Henchard's mood of gloomy jealousy has been satisfied, but the following morning he regrets what he has said. Matters are made worse when he discovers 'that this time Farfrae was determined to take him at his word'. Again, Henchard's impulsive behaviour has furthered his own decline.

CHAPTER XVII, *pp. 180–86*

Elizabeth-Jane knows she has displeased her father by dancing with Farfrae. She is embarrassed and miserable about this and, as she thinks about it, she meets Farfrae. He tells her that he is leaving her father's employment. It is clear that the two young people are fond of each other, indeed, Farfrae even hints at marriage. That Elizabeth-Jane is distressed by his imminent departure is made touchingly clear (p. 182).

But Farfrae does not leave Casterbridge. He buys out the small business of one of Henchard's rivals and thus sets up as a direct competitor. Elizabeth-Jane is delighted he is staying and tries to guess how much he may love her (p. 183).

Henchard is furious at Farfrae's move and his old, violent temper shows through clearly. His somewhat high-handed treatment of his fellow town councillors does not invite them to be deeply sympathetic. He goes out of their meeting alone and, on returning home, he finds Elizabeth-Jane. He bluntly refuses to allow her to see Farfrae again and writes a note to him to that effect. As Hardy points out (p. 185) Henchard has here failed to take advantage of the situation because of his headstrong nature. A marriage between the young people would have eased Henchard's relations with Farfrae. Henchard's diplomacy, Hardy comments, 'was as wrong-headed as a buffalo's'. This is a powerful and just image.

For his part, Farfrae is determined not to antagonize Henchard. The older man has been his friend and he does not want to hurt him. This is entirely decent, though Farfrae's decision 'to enact no Romeo part towards Elizabeth-Jane' shows how calculating he can be.

It is this power to calculate which makes Farfrae a successful man.

He is the opposite of the moody and impulsive Henchard (p. 185). It is inevitable that 'a time came when, avoid collision with his former friend as he might, Forfrae was compelled, in sheer self-defence, to close with Henchard in mortal commercial combat'. What we shall witness is the clash of two temperaments, of the old 'rule o' thumb' world of Henchard and the modern, scientific approach of Farfrae. Two forces, two characters, are in opposition and 'Character' as Hardy writes, quoting Novalis 'is Fate'. There is no need to think that Fate is any more kind or less impulsive than Henchard himself.

CHAPTER XVIII, *pp. 187–91*

We learn first that Susan is ill and then, more dramatically, we are introduced to Lucetta. This introduction, as with so many destructive things in *The Mayor of Casterbridge*, is effected through a letter.

Lucetta appears as the forgiving woman. She understands Henchard's position and all she requires from him is the return of her letters. Nonetheless, she insists that Henchard hand these to her in person. She has no intention of allowing him the simple expedient of posting the letters back to her.

But this is a chapter full of letters and we should know by now that these always portend tragedy. Just as Henchard makes his way to see Lucetta and return her letters to her, so Susan, his dying wife, also scribbles a final note. We are not told what it says. That it contains shattering revelations will only be known later.

Elizabeth-Jane sits with her mother who rouses herself for one more revelation. Yet again it concerns notes, this time the notes Farfrae and Elizabeth-Jane received which threw them alone together for the first time. It was Susan who wrote them: she wanted Elizabeth-Jane and Farfrae to marry. By her own light, she had acted for the best. The passive little woman had taken yet another initiative. However, Fate had not let things go as she wished. Her dying comment (p. 190) expresses thwarted hope and the hidden truths that only time will reveal. As such, it is almost a summary of the whole novel.

The comments of the rustics on Susan's death are both richly amusing and deeply poetic, particularly the last comments of Mother Cuxsom. However, her comment that Susan is 'helpless to hinder . . . anything now' gives the feeling that the bitter hidden truths will be ruthlessly revealed. The cupboards will indeed be opened and they will contain skeletons beyond all imagining.

CHAPTER XIX, *pp. 192–9*

Three weeks after Susan's funeral her husband and daughter are sitting by the fire. They start to talk and Henchard is hurt by Elizabeth-Jane's thinking of Newson as her father. He asks her how she would view him if he were her father. To the girl the idea is inconceivable. However, Henchard presses on. He is lonely. He has lost his wife and the friendship of Farfrae. He wants to establish firmly his relationship with his daughter. Eventually he tells Elizabeth-Jane the truth – or, at least, the truth as he knows it. Elizabeth-Jane is his daughter. She, naturally, is deeply upset but she agrees to change her surname and Henchard offers to show her papers to prove her parentage. This is deeply ironic for the paper he finds when he goes to search is Susan's last letter. Despite the superscription: '*Not to be opened till Elizabeth-Jane's wedding day*' the feeble Susan had failed to seal the letter properly: 'her seal had cracked, and the letter was open'. This sort of irony delighted Hardy. Naturally, Henchard reads the letter and, of course, it tells him that Elizabeth-Jane is Newson's child after all. His own daughter is dead. Henchard is stunned.

The workings of Fate, Chance and tragic irony are clear here and we may single this moment out as central to Hardy's whole vision. Henchard abused Susan and she left him. Her departure left Henchard free to realize his potential. He has become a great and powerful man, but subject to loneliness and impulsive moods. Nineteen years later his naïve but remorseless wife returns to him bringing with her an attractive young woman. Susan's only wish is for the good of Elizabeth-Jane. For her sake she 'remarries' Henchard and pushes forward her daughter's affair with Henchard's manager Farfrae. Feeble herself, she has entangled Henchard in a web of lies. However, she has meant well. This is an example of that 'honesty in dishonesty which had characterized her in other things'. That her letter falls open and the best of her intentions are betrayed is an example of that cruel and gratuitous irony that characterizes the novel as a whole.

Henchard looks at his 'daughter' and sees her physical similarities to Newson. Both his anger and his superstition are aroused: 'he could not help thinking that the concatenation of events this evening had produced was the scheme of some sinister intelligence bent on punishing him' (p. 197). The part of Casterbridge Henchard now wanders through is described in sinister terms, but the tragic dilemma in which Henchard finds himself is powerfully suggested.

Henchard is determined, however, that Elizabeth-Jane will keep his name. He is too 'self-willed' to back down on this. He returns home from his lonely, anguished walk. And now one of the most moving moments in the book takes place. Elizabeth-Jane has thought all night about what her father has told her and finally she joyfully accepts him as her father indeed. Her goodwill flows out to him. The tender description of Henchard's response is beautifully written. The situation in which Henchard finds himself is highly contrived and even artificial, but the very real human feelings the situation inspires could not be more clear or more satisfyingly stated (p. 199).

CHAPTER XX, *pp. 200–209*

Elizabeth-Jane is confused. Her 'father' at first welcomed her as his 'daughter'. Now he is cold, even harsh, to her (p. 200). His criticism of her takes the form of chiding her vulgarities of speech and her accomplishments. It is ironic that Henchard himself is 'uncultivated'. The climax of this comes when Henchard catches Elizabeth-Jane bringing a cup of ale to Nance Mockridge. Henchard is furious that Elizabeth-Jane should so lower herself, but Nance Mockridge, in bitter retort, tells Henchard how Elizabeth-Jane once served in the Three Mariners. Henchard feels this threatens his self-made status and he is now cruelly cold to Elizabeth-Jane. She, for her part, tries to improve herself with reading: 'mastering facts with painful laboriousness, but never flinching from her self-imposed task'. Her effort is moving and a way of suppressing her love for Farfrae (p. 204). Elizabeth-Jane lives on, 'a dumb, deep-feeling, great-eyed creature'.

One day she goes to visit her mother's grave. To her amazement she finds another woman there: indeed, a lady. Elizabeth-Jane is suitably impressed. The atmosphere is appropriately sinister but, as yet, the two women have not spoken.

Henchard, meanwhile, has learnt two things: that he is not to be made an alderman and that it was none other than Farfrae that Elizabeth-Jane waited on in the Three Mariners. He now realizes that the decline in his fortunes set in the moment his wife and Elizabeth-Jane came to Casterbridge. The dramatic irony that impressed us with the force of art is now felt in all its bitterness by Henchard. Susan herself is dead, Henchard now wants to get rid of Elizabeth-Jane. He tries to lure Farfrae into marrying her.

Elizabeth-Jane visits her mother's grave a second time. She briefly sees Farfrae but then sits down and expresses her despair aloud. She thinks she is alone, but she is not. The fashionable lady has heard her cry and comes forward to comfort her. They discuss Henchard and Elizabeth-Jane's personal history. The kindly lady offers Elizabeth-Jane the post of her companion. Elizabeth-Jane is overwhelmed. Happiness, and with it social and cultural advance, seem to be opening up for her. Fate and Chance seem suddenly kind and she will be lonely no more. You should note how loneliness and the attempt to escape from it are dominant themes in *The Mayor of Casterbridge*. We should be more wary, however, for the 'lady', of course, is none other than Henchard's mistress: Lucetta. Coincidence will embroil all the characters in yet further tragic ironies.

CHAPTER XXI, *pp. 210–17*

High-Place Hall, Lucetta's home, becomes an obsession to Elizabeth-Jane, and she goes to look at it. Significantly, the house overlooks the market place. This will provide further drama. It also suggests the near connection between the 'great house' and what it implies and the 'trade' in which both Henchard and Farfrae are involved.

Elizabeth-Jane leaves the site of the house, but, as she does so, is unaware that the house is about to receive another visitor: Henchard. Neither has seen the other, but on their return Elizabeth-Jane informs Henchard that she has been offered the post of lady's companion. She does not mention who this lady is or where she lives. Henchard is only too pleased to be rid of Elizabeth-Jane and offers her money. His disinterest in her is clear from his refusal to ask her any questions about the job she has been offered. Elizabeth-Jane goes off, meets Lucetta, and tells her that her father has agreed to their plan. The woman is pleased but their conversation is interrupted by voices from the other side of a wall. One voice is Henchard's. Lucetta is distracted by it but, coming to herself again, suggests that Elizabeth-Jane come to her at six o'clock and should not discuss the matter further with her father. Her own name, she informs the girl, is Miss Templeman. The whole scene, its setting and dialogue, is loaded with suspicion and intrigue.

Henchard is surprised by the rapidity of Elizabeth-Jane's departure (p. 216). He feels hurt but responds gruffly until he sees how Elizabeth-Jane has been trying to improve herself. Then he is touched. As so often in the novel, Henchard tries to change his violent mood. He wants his 'daughter' back. His offer comes 'ten minutes too late'. She wants to leave and Henchard will be left alone. As she departs she innocently tells him where she is going. Henchard is frozen in horror.

CHAPTER XXII, *pp. 218–28*

Lucetta has indeed established herself in Casterbridge. As she informs Henchard, now that Susan is dead it is reasonable for her to hope their relationship may prosper. The previous evening the lonely man had been to see her, but he had not realized that she was calling herself Miss Templeman and so supposed that Lucetta had not yet arrived (p. 219). This confusion suggests something of Henchard's naïvety. It also strongly suggests Lucetta's fickle and devious nature. A second note, however, clears up all doubt. Lucetta has inherited property from an aunt and taken her name. With money she is her own mistress and has 'chosen to reside in Casterbridge'. She then explains that the advantage of having Elizabeth-Jane live with her is that Henchard himself will frequently be able to come and visit the house without raising suspicion. Henchard is well pleased. He goes to High-Place Hall but is politely refused entrance. Lucetta is otherwise engaged.

We now see Lucetta and Elizabeth-Jane together. It is clear from the start that Lucetta is a sensuous and sophisticated creature (p. 221) while Elizabeth-Jane's relative naïvety is again established (p. 222). Lucetta tells her something of her past. It is, we note, a carefully edited version. There is no detailing of her time in Jersey, for example.

It is clear that Lucetta is still fond of Henchard. As the two women look out over the market-place they both see their respective loves: Henchard and Farfrae. Elizabeth-Jane denies she has a particular interest in any of the men out in the market and eventually confesses that the reason why Henchard does not visit them is the quarrel they have had. At this, Lucetta 'bursts into hysterical sobs'. What had seemed such an 'ingenious scheme' has completely foundered. She contrives to have Elizabeth-Jane leave the house for a few hours (p. 227) and then sends one of her many notes to Henchard informing him of how she has arranged things.

It is clear that Lucetta no longer deeply loves Henchard, however. His refusal to visit her has cooled her feelings and her chief desire now is more business-like than anything else: 'there remained a conscientious wish to bring about her union with him'. Nonetheless, when she does hear a man's step, she is highly excited. She turns to greet him, but 'the man before her was not Henchard'.

CHAPTER XXIII, *pp. 229–36*

The man is Farfrae, come to see Elizabeth-Jane. Lucetta, of course, is immediately attracted to him. To the unfolding ironies of the past are now added the ironies of present love affairs.

Farfrae has come to woo Elizabeth-Jane; he has the money to marry her if he chooses. Such a marriage looks like a sound business proposition. Elizabeth-Jane is solid and reliable and the marriage might well repair Farfrae's relations with her father. However, it is clear that Lucetta finds Farfrae sexually attractive and she flirts with him while he tells her how successful in business he has been. Indeed, the business man in Farfrae is always near the surface, but Lucetta detects that he does not lack a sentimental side. She plays on his love for Scotland which, right from our first introduction to him, has been the subject by which his emotions are most easily roused. However, the pathetic sight of two lovers in the market-place about to part stirs both Lucetta and Farfrae, and the latter goes out to arrange things so that they are kept together. It is a generous gesture but it has clearly been made on Lucetta's inspiration. Even as he returns to her, Farfrae realizes he has been uncharacteristically weak (p. 234). He then realizes that business is calling him back to the market-place. He is reluctant to go. Both the man and the older woman realize they have begun to fall in love. As Hardy comments, 'She had enkindled the young man's enthusiasm until he was quite brimming with senti-ment; while he, from merely affording her a new form of idleness had gone on to wake her serious solicitude'.

The love that is awoken here is both tender and dangerous; the ironies are deep and potentially tragic. The man who had called to see Elizabeth-Jane has fallen in love with Lucetta. She, waiting for Hen-chard, has fallen in love with his enemy. Now, when Henchard calls on her she does not wish to see him. Hardy comments that she had quickened Henchard's feelings but that she was now indifferent to the achievement. She will keep on Elizabeth-Jane for, under the circumstances, she will be a useful means of keeping Henchard at bay. The speed and drama of the ironies that Hardy creates could hardly be neater.

Perhaps the greatest irony of all is that the reader actually enjoys Hardy's skill, enjoys seeing the characters in the novel involved in such elegantly-constructed tragedy.

CHAPTER XXIV, *pp. 237–45*

Elizabeth-Jane, unaware of what has happened, is delighted that she can remain with Lucetta. From the house she can watch the business of the market, watch for Farfrae. Indeed, this is what both women do (p. 237).

New clothes arrive for the women. They dress and prepare yet again to watch the market-place. They witness the arrival of a 'seed-drill', an implement of the new, advanced agriculture. Both women realize that Farfrae must be responsible for it. Initiative in love and business comes now from him rather than Henchard. The women, like everyone else in Casterbridge, find the machine fascinating and they go out to see it, or, more accurately, its introducer. The man they meet, of course, is Henchard.

Lucetta and Henchard play the charade of not knowing each other in front of Elizabeth-Jane. From Henchard's comments (p. 239) it is clear what he thinks of Farfrae, but he resists being too rude, remembering that the 'jumped-up jackanapes' may well be courting his daughter. This, of course, would be to his advantage. Some words are exchanged between Henchard and Lucetta which are half overheard by Elizabeth-Jane. She is confused by them. They seem to imply some relationship between her supposed father and Lucetta. However, the sound of a ballad sung from inside the new machine introduces us to Farfrae who now becomes the personification of efficient, modern agriculture. The machine, he reveals, is a great invention. There will be no more waste. Elizabeth-Jane's comment (p. 240) shows how the poetry, the human sentiment of farming, is giving way to a mechanized society. Inevitably, this is also a comment about Farfrae and all he stands for. He himself is not wholly unappreciative of Elizabeth-Jane's sadness but he bows before the Progress he has himself introduced. The scene is a high point in Hardy's discussion of the theme of the new versus the old. Hardy is too subtle a writer to come down finally on one side or the other, but it is easy to see where his feelings lie.

The emotion between Farfrae and Lucetta is detected even by Elizabeth-Jane, although she is unsure what it may signify. Lucetta is somewhat patronizing to her but their evening conversation is full of irony (p. 242), an irony that the 'discerning silent' Elizabeth-Jane begins to unravel as, indeed, she does again when Lucetta gives her a veiled account of her own history. Elizabeth-Jane is beginning to grow up, to be matured by the world of adult duplicity in which she is an only half-conscious victim.

CHAPTER XXV, *pp. 246–51*

Farfrae is replacing Henchard in Lucetta's affections and the person who suffers most is Elizabeth-Jane as she sees the growing and changing emotions of the man she loves. Wrongly, she believes that Farfrae is the man whom Lucetta had described as her lover at the end of the previous chapter. She is already beginning to adopt the stoical philosophy that will be her greatest strength (p. 246).

Henchard, meanwhile, is still in love with Lucetta and he eventually overcomes his pride sufficiently to call on her for a second time. He now feels inferior before her and her new wealth. Nonetheless, he proposes marriage. Lucetta answers evasively, but in the ensuing heated conversation it becomes clear that Henchard is worried by the possibility of gossip and that Lucetta has no intention of encouraging his suit.

Left to herself, Lucetta determines to love Farfrae and reject Henchard utterly. This is a purely emotional reaction, a sudden, uncalculated decision. Lucetta is a woman on her own. Her priorities are love and an easy life. Lucetta, as Hardy says, 'with native lightness of heart took kindly to what fate offered'. Such frivolity will not mean that the Fate she casually embraces will be kind to her.

It is, of course, Elizabeth-Jane who chiefly suffers, by being ignored (p. 250) by her 'father', her sometime lover and the woman who was once her friend. Elizabeth-Jane is a shrewd observer, and this only increases her suffering. She realizes the difference of nature between Henchard's and Farfrae's love for Lucetta, but she also begins to take on something else: a modest, humble acceptance of a world where hope is thwarted and what is unwanted is what we get. The naïve, simple girl is developing a strength and stoicism which make her strong if not obviously attractive. The last paragraph of this chapter is a moving statement of how, if life is to be endured, a certain dignity must be achieved. This is the voice of quietly reasoned suffering to be contrasted to the dramatic anguish of the other leading characters.

CHAPTER XXVI, *pp. 252–62*

Henchard and Farfrae meet. Henchard tells him of his predicament but Farfrae does not realize that the woman his former friend is describing is none other than Lucetta, his present mistress. This comforts Henchard. He had begun to be suspicious of Farfrae and Lucetta.

Nonetheless, Henchard knows he has a rival in love and questions Lucetta as to whether it might be Farfrae. No sooner is the topic broached than Farfrae joins them for tea (p. 253). The embarrassment is mutual and Henchard's suspicions deepen. Only Elizabeth-Jane can see the incident as 'ridiculous'.

To this rivalry in love is added Henchard's and Farfrae's rivalry in business. To help secure his position, Henchard now employs Jopp as a manager. He, of course, is the man whose job Farfrae had taken at the start of the novel. The wheel has almost turned full circle. But what is most important to note is that Jopp 'was the only one in Casterbridge besides Henchard and the close-lipped Elizabeth who knew that Lucetta came truly from Jersey'. This knowledge makes Jopp a dangerous man.

Henchard confides to Jopp that he wants to destroy Farfrae 'by fair competition'. Jopp, of course, is more than willing to help remove his former rival. He recognizes Farfrae's luck in business but agrees to help Henchard 'under-sell him, and over-buy him, and so snuff him out'. Only Elizabeth-Jane, yet again the silent and unseen observer, is aware that Jopp is the wrong man for the job (p. 256).

Hardy now explains something of the financial background to the wheat business (see pp. 256–7). The harvest is very much the victim of the forces of Nature, of Fate. The result is a deep feeling of powerlessness on the part of the old-fashioned rustics. Henchard gambles on the weather ruining the crops, and the superstitious 'fetishistic' side to his personality that we saw when he swore his oath to renounce drink resurfaces. Henchard, showing clearly what an unscientific man he is, goes to consult a 'weather prophet' (p. 258). Hardy relishes the superstitious atmosphere here and it is highly dramatic. Equally, it is in important contrast to Farfrae's scientific approach to farming. The 'weather-prophet' speaks in a suitably 'magical' way and forecasts tempestuous rain in the last fortnight of August. Henchard is sufficiently taken in. The man has supported his own ideas and so he is willing to believe him. Henchard buys vast quantities of grain at a high price, hoping, of course, to sell it at a yet higher price when the harvests are spoiled. The weather does indeed change. Suddenly the days are full of bright sunshine. The harvest, needless to say, is excellent and 'prices rushed down'. As a result, Henchard loses a great deal of money as he sells his wheat in a panic. His gamble with the weather, supposedly backed by sound advice, has not paid off. The indifferent and even malevolent forces of Nature could not be made more clear. As Henchard knows, speculation of the sort he has made must be in the nature of a gamble. He has gambled and lost. As a result, he is obliged to mortgage much of his property. His financial ruin is now imminent.

As he comes out from his humiliating meeting at the bank, Henchard meets Jopp. The two men argue. Henchard blames Jopp for his predicament and, in the heat of the moment, Henchard sacks him.

CHAPTER XXVII, *pp. 263–71*

Farfrae is buying up corn at what he knows to be far too cheap a price. Like Henchard, he is speculating, gambling. Unlike Henchard, of course, his gambling will be hugely successful. He will have at his disposal large stores of wheat while Henchard, who has tried to sell as much of his expensively bought corn as possible, will have none. If the weather does change and the harvest is ruined then Farfrae will have abundant supplies which he can sell at a great profit. Of course, the weather changes.

In view of Farfrae's success, Henchard now begins to wonder if he is the victim of black magic (p. 263). His superstitious nature is again manifest. Farfrae, on the other hand, prospers and is likely soon to be made mayor.

The rivalry between them and Farfrae's superior position is made clear by the incident with the two wagons (pp. 264–5). Henchard's sheer ill luck and Farfrae's attractiveness to women are strongly brought out here. The brief conversation with the 'old constable' is the first hint of yet another humiliation in store for Henchard.

The town is behind with its harvesting and so the people are working by moonlight. Farfrae and Lucetta, observed by Henchard, go out to watch them. Henchard, unobserved, listens to them talk. Their love for each other is obvious. When Lucetta and Farfrae part, Henchard follows her home. An anguished conversation takes place in which Lucetta confesses that she had thought she should marry Henchard, not because she loved him, but for 'conscience' sake' (p. 269). Now that she is truly in love, and with someone else, her conscience is a less compelling force. She begs Henchard to leave her

(p. 270). He, for his part, threatens to expose their past and so ruin Lucetta's chances with Farfrae unless she agrees to marry him that night. We see Henchard here in a very poor light indeed. Indeed, this is the blackmail of a desperate man, but, for the sake of his own dignity, Henchard simply cannot allow his successful rival in business to rival him successfully in love. Elizabeth-Jane is summoned in and she is forced to witness Lucetta's pathetic agreement to her marriage with Henchard. Elizabeth-Jane tries to protect Lucetta from doing what so clearly distresses her, but to no avail. As Henchard callously comments, what he has done will leave Farfrae free for Elizabeth-Jane.

Henchard now leaves and Elizabeth-Jane is utterly bewildered by the scene she has witnessed. How can Lucetta and her father know each other so well? What secrets have been hidden from her?

CHAPTER XXVIII, *pp. 272–6*

Henchard is threatened financially and in his love life. We have just seen him behave with gross injustice. The circumstances of his present life are in turmoil; now the chaos of his past will catch up with him as well. Indeed, they will join forces to destroy the man.

Despite this, Henchard is still a magistrate. That he would have to preside at a trial was briefly mentioned in the previous chapter (p. 266). The repulsive creature on whom he has to pass judgement, however, is none other than the furmity-woman. As she is about to be sentenced she responds in the meanest way. She is well aware of the irony and injustice of being sentenced by Henchard and so she exposes him, revealing the guilty and sordid details of his past (p. 274). As she rightly declares, her story 'proves that he's no better than I, and has no right to sit there in judgement upon me'. With great dignity, Henchard admits that the woman is right. The effect on the court and the crowd that has gathered outside is sensational.

Now, for the first time, Lucetta hears the truth of Henchard's separation from his wife. The revelation is a social disgrace and she is bitter that it should concern the man she has so recently been forced to agree to marry. She decides that the only thing she can do is to go away for a few days. When she returns, Henchard calls for her, but is told that she has gone for a walk. Neither Henchard nor the reader knows at this point that, in her absence, Lucetta and Farfrae have married.

CHAPTER XXIX, *pp. 277–85*

Lucetta, out walking, sighs for Farfrae. She has, of course, an appointment with him. She turns round but is greeted not by him but by Elizabeth-Jane. The two women, alone in the countryside, are suddenly threatened by a rampant bull, and are only saved at the last moment by a man, none other than Henchard. Seen in this detached way, the incident may seem faintly ridiculous. In fact, in the context of the novel, it is both a powerful description and an image suggesting how both women are threatened in their emotional lives. Henchard's actions also serve to reveal his still very considerable physical power. He will eventually be defeated and crushed, but a man of this force will not easily be overcome.

At this moment, Farfrae too appears. His concern for Lucetta's well-being is clear. So is his calculating nature. He allows Lucetta and Henchard to be alone. 'Henchard had saved Lucetta, and to provoke a possible exhibition of her deeper affection for himself was as ungenerous as it was unwise' (p. 281). When Farfrae returns home, we are informed that he is about to move house. At first, this seems rather confusing, rather unnecessary. It is only later, when we are told of his marriage, that we realize he is in the process of moving to Lucetta's house.

Lucetta loves Farfrae, whom she has secretly married, but she has been saved by his rival Henchard whom she had once promised to marry. This irony causes much suffering. Nonetheless, Lucetta asks Henchard how she can thank him for rescuing her. She is now a rich woman and Henchard asks her to tell his chief creditor that they are indeed to wed. This will buy Henchard time and so ease his financial position. Henchard's desperation here is obvious and he cannot understand Lucetta's reluctance to help him when it is so easily in her power. Eventually she is forced to confess: she is already married to Farfrae and none other than Henchard's creditor, Mr Grower, was the witness to the ceremony. As Lucetta makes her tearful confession to the 'idiotized' Henchard they hear the bells and town band bursting out in celebration. Henchard appreciates the bitter irony of saving his rival's wife, but when she offers still to advance him the money, he refuses it. His pride forbids him to be 'a pensioner of Farfrae's wife'.

CHAPTER XXX, *pp. 286–90*

Farfrae is moving to High-Place Hall. No one, needless to say, has informed Elizabeth-Jane. Lucetta agrees to tell her the news and asks Farfrae to let the girl stay on with her. This is an innocent kindness on Lucetta's part. That Farfrae is unaware of the suffering it must inevitably cause Elizabeth-Jane reveals how shallow his concern for other people really is.

Elizabeth-Jane now has to be told the truth. She has some idea of what is happening to Lucetta. She knows, for example, that the 'first man' in the story she tells her is her own father. She tries to defend his rights and for a moment almost believes that Lucetta has indeed married him (p. 289). Then the truth dawns on her: 'You – have – married Mr Farfrae!' She asks to be left alone. Her decision is instantly made: she must leave. She cannot live in the same house as the two people who have so abused her and the man she believes to be her father. As Hardy comments, 'her craving for correctness of procedure was, indeed, almost vicious'. Elizabeth-Jane packs her belongings and silently disappears to live in rented rooms and survive on what money Henchard has provided for her and on what little she can earn.

One matter that interests the locals is what Farfrae will now do.

CHAPTER XXXI, *pp. 291–5*

The other matter that interests the rustics is the revelation of Henchard's past. The last third of the book is concerned with his destruction. The trial of the furmity-woman marks the beginning of this.

When Henchard tried the woman we saw that he was already facing financial trouble of a great order. We saw too, and have since had confirmed, that his hopes of love have been utterly dashed. The present holds nothing for him. It has been wrecked by a combination of bad luck and sheer impulsiveness. Henchard has only his past left to him and in that lies his certain destruction. Again, it is sheer bad luck that the furmity-woman should expose him when she does. It is significant that what she exposes is the scandalous story of Henchard's impulsive past. There is now no one to whom Henchard can turn. He is set for tragedy:

> Small as the police-court incident had been in itself, it formed the edge or turn in the incline of Henchard's fortunes. On that day – almost at that minute – he passed the ridge of prosperity and honour, and began to descend rapidly on the other side. It was strange how soon he sank in esteem. Socially he had received a startling fillip downwards; and having already lost commercial buoyancy from rash transactions, the velocity of his descent in both aspects became accelerated every hour.

More catastrophies indeed accumulate. Just as when we saw Henchard in triumph he was threatened by the 'growed-wheat', so now, as he falls, he is caught out again (p. 291). It is not his fault, but he must take the blame. And then, suddenly, we learn that he is bankrupt (p. 292). Movingly, Henchard offers his creditors even his gold watch. That Henchard has been transparently honest in defeat is recognized by all. His virtue increasingly shines through his ever-deepening tragedy. To emphasize this, Hardy shows us Henchard selling the watch to pay off one of his small creditors who would otherwise have suffered from his bankruptcy. Even the mean-minded rustics have to admire the one quality – his energy – which had caused Henchard to rise. But it is safe to admire the man now that he has fallen.

Henchard takes refuge with Jopp, the man whom he had 'employed, abused, cajoled and dismissed by turns'. In his defeat, Henchard refuses to see Elizabeth-Jane, the one person who really cares for him.

In Casterbridge Henchard's name is obliterated. Farfrae buys up the bankrupt business. He hires Henchard's old labourers at a shilling a week less than Henchard paid them. They accept this. Farfrae at least provides them with regular, untroubled work. They are glad to be rid of Henchard's impulsive temper. Life is ordered now. The new scientific world has taken over. A man emotionally far poorer has become rich at Henchard's expense and 'the scales and steel-yards began to be busy where guesswork had formerly been the rule'.

CHAPTER XXXII, *pp. 296–303*

Henchard goes to the two bridges in Casterbridge where 'gravitated all the failure of the town'. He learns from Jopp that Farfrae has not only bought his house but all Henchard's furniture too. When Jopp leaves, Farfrae himself appears. He has heard that Henchard is thinking of emigrating, just as Farfrae himself was at the start of the book. Farfrae offers Henchard rooms in his house. The wheel, as both men realize, has turned full circle (p. 299). Henchard, of course, refuses the offer; neither does he accept Farfrae's offer of the return of some of his furniture.

Elizabeth-Jane's lodgings are opposite her 'father's' old house, now the home of her former friend, Lucetta, and of her one time lover, Farfrae. She learns that Henchard has caught a cold and is determined to see him. The effects of her strong-willed kindness are made clear (p. 301). Henchard eventually recovers sufficient strength to go to Farfrae and ask for a job as a labourer, 'a journeyman hay-trusser'. The foreman accepts Henchard on behalf of Farfrae, who cannot bring himself to deal with the man personally. Henchard is back where he began and 'the once flourishing merchant and Mayor and what not stood as a day-labourer in the barns and granaries he had formerly owned'. The tragic irony is stark and its pathos is underlined by the appearance of Henchard's working clothes (p. 302).

Naturally, it is rumoured that Farfrae will become mayor and Henchard puts this down to Lucetta's money. The cruel ironies of his life play on Henchard's mind. He begins to mutter ominously to himself and then, when the day of his twenty-one-year vow not to drink is up, Elizabeth-Jane hears that, 'Michael Henchard have busted out drinking after taking nothing for twenty-one years!'

CHAPTER XXXIII, *pp. 304–11*

'The flush upon his face proclaimed at once that the vow of twenty-one years had lapsed, and the era of recklessness begun anew.' Henchard is in the Three Mariners, the pub where he met Farfrae, the instrument of his downfall. Henchard is drunk and bids the sober musicians strike up a tune. As he is choosing a psalm, Henchard looks up to see 'Mr Councillor Farfrae with Lucetta upon his arm'. To the embarrassment of the musicians, Henchard chooses Psalm 109 whose words are bitterly appropriate (p. 306). Drunk, Henchard is furious at the musicians' refusal to sing and play. Eventually they are persuaded to do so. As they finish, Farfrae and Lucetta pass by again. Henchard declares that the words of the psalm have been directed at Farfrae. They are, of course, far more appropriate to Henchard.

Henchard is rescued by Elizabeth-Jane who is alarmed by his threats to Farfrae. They go to Jopp's cottage but Henchard refuses to let Elizabeth-Jane in.

She, for her part, continues wisely observing relations between Farfrae and Lucetta and begins also to help her father (p. 309).

Eventually Henchard and Lucetta meet. The woman does not know that Henchard is working for her husband and Henchard exploits this with bitter sarcasm (p. 310). As a result, Lucetta writes another of her notes, this time requesting Henchard not to be so cruel. Henchard burns it, but the pressures of his life cause him to drink ever more deeply. Elizabeth-Jane thinks that he might be planning to murder Farfrae (p. 311) and resolves to warn him.

CHAPTER XXXIV, *pp. 312–20*

Elizabeth-Jane rises early to warn Farfrae about Henchard but the Scot at first refuses to take her seriously. He resolves, instead, to buy Henchard a little seedsman's shop. This decision shows Farfrae to have previously been more unimaginative than heartless in his dealings with Henchard. He needs to be prompted by people with fuller hearts. However, when he hears of the vengeance Henchard has been swearing, he drops his plan. The owner of the shop tells Henchard, 'that a scheme of the Council for setting him up . . . had been knocked on the head by Farfrae'. Hardy comments, 'and thus out of error enmity grew', (p. 314).

Farfrae is hurt by Henchard's reactions; he is not imaginative enough to understand them. Of course, he does not know of Lucetta's past affair with Henchard, but he comments that Henchard's behaviour 'is more like old-fashioned rivalry in love than just a bit of rivalry in trade'. This is both ironic and a revelation of Farfrae's own values. Trade is his measure of all things. Lucetta is clearly in distress and wants to leave Casterbridge.

Farfrae is now asked to become mayor. His victory is all but complete. At this moment of triumph, secured largely by his own efforts, he exclaims:

See now how it's ourselves that are ruled by the Powers above us! We plan this, but we do that. If they want to make me Mayor I will stay, and Henchard must rave as he will.

At the moment when the townspeople are celebrating Farfrae's election, Lucetta asks Henchard for the return of her old love letters. Suddenly Henchard has the means of revenge at his disposal. It is highly likely that the papers were left in the wall safe of his former home. He asks if he may look for them and arrives drunkenly that evening to do so. He finds the letters, informs Farfrae in a general way that they are from his 'other woman' and derives great pleasure from Farfrae's ignorance and the bitter, ironic things he causes the young man to say about the woman, about Lucetta, his own wife. The reader, of course, is waiting for Henchard to reveal the truth. That, indeed, is what he had intended to do. But Hardy is more subtle a writer than this. He wants us to be moved by Henchard's nobility and he makes Henchard change his mind. The hero cannot bring himself to wreck his enemy's marriage. Farfrae is newly Mayor of Casterbridge, he has acquired Henchard's business, he has married the woman Henchard loves. There is every reason for Henchard to destroy him. He does not do so because 'such a wrecking of hearts appalled even him'.

CHAPTER XXXV, *pp. 321–5*

Lucetta overhears Henchard reading her letters to Farfrae. This worries her terribly but she is greatly relieved when she realizes that Henchard has not revealed who wrote them. Nonetheless, in her worry, Lucetta writes a note to Henchard begging him to meet her at the Ring and assure her that he will 'carry this horse-play no further'.

She goes out, veiled and drably dressed, to her appointment at the Ring, that place where Henchard met Susan when she returned and which we know to be the place least propitious to happy lovers. Henchard himself is fully aware of this and mollified by it (p. 323). He begins to feel ashamed of himself and loses all his desire to humiliate Lucetta. He agrees to hand back the letters but warns Lucetta that the truth is almost bound to be discovered. Of course it will be, but the means by which Henchard and Lucetta's past becomes the subject of common gossip is bizarre in the extreme.

CHAPTER XXXVI, *pp. 326–35*

Lucetta returns from her meeting and encounters Jopp. He asks her to
help secure him a job with Farfrae and, more significantly, mentions
that he knew her in Jersey. He then returns to his own house where
Henchard asks him to deliver Lucetta's old love letters to her. Jopp
realizes that the letters concern Henchard but, as he goes to deliver
them, is persuaded by some rustics to visit an inn in a poor, dishonest
area (p. 327). Among the customers at the inn is the furmity-woman. She
asks Jopp about his parcel of letters. He does not explain directly, but it
is clear from what he says that he wants his revenge on Lucetta for what
he thinks is the highhanded way she has just dealt with him. The letters
are opened and read and it becomes increasingly clear that Lucetta wrote
them. To the rustics, Lucetta's behaviour seems a good reason for
holding a 'skimmity-ride', the public punishment of adultery by par-
ading an image of the victims noisily through the town. The rustics are
encouraged in this by the chance arrival of a stranger. When Lucetta
finally receives the letters the next day, she burns them. She is, of
course, too late to save herself from public humiliation.

CHAPTER XXXVII, *pp. 336–42*

Simultaneous with the excitement over the skimmington is that
produced by the prospect of the visit to Casterbridge of a 'Royal
Personage'. This will be a great occasion. Henchard desperately wishes
to join his old companions on the Council in welcoming the visitor,
but Farfrae has to refuse him (p. 337). Henchard meets Elizabeth-
Jane and tells her that, now he is drinking again, he can find the
courage to welcome the royal visitor in his own right. He kits himself out with a flag and rosette (p. 338), but still looks pathetically
shabby.

Farfrae and Lucetta are, of course, on show. The 'Royal Personage'
is about to arrive. Henchard steps out in front of his coach but is
removed by Farfrae. The royal visit takes place despite some mild

embarrassment. Lucetta is particularly embarrassed by some comments from those next to her. The rustics, however, resenting the triumph of Lucetta and her husband, are yet more resolved to go ahead with the skimmington. They are determined to humble the pair. Hardy makes it clear that now Farfrae is a successful man he has lost the glamour he once held for the poorest people (p. 342). They realize how the skimmington will be a bitterly dramatic 'wind-up to the Royal visit'.

CHAPTER XXXVIII, *pp. 343–9*

The Royal visit has brought Lucetta 'a great triumph', even if it is too brief.

Henchard, meanwhile, is annoyed that his plan has failed and meets with Jopp who tells him of his own disappointment at Lucetta's hand. Henchard largely ignores him but is determined to have his own revenge on Farfrae. He resolves to fight him. As the bigger man, he ties his left arm behind him and lies in wait for his enemy. They meet and fight (pp. 345–6). Henchard, naturally, gets Farfrae at his mercy. His moment for pure revenge has come. We have seen Henchard's great physical strength; now we see his human kindness. He lets Farfrae go (p. 348) and is bitterly ashamed of himself and his plan. His emotional impetuosity is clear. He wants now to apologize, but he realizes that Farfrae is out of town (p. 349). As he waits for Farfrae to return, he hears but takes no notice of the sounds of the skimmington.

CHAPTER XXXIX, *pp. 350–57*

Farfrae has been sent out of Casterbridge on a wild goose chase by the organizers of the skimmington. Towards Lucetta they have no such compassion. As she hears the 'ride' approaching, Elizabeth-Jane comes to her. The girl tries to protect Lucetta from the sight, but to no avail. Lucetta is mortified for herself and terrified that Farfrae will see the procession too. Indeed, the sight makes her all but hysterical. She faints, and the doctor declares her to be in a serious state of shock. Lucetta, we will discover, is pregnant. The doctor urgently summons Farfrae. Mr Grower (the witness to Lucetta's wedding) tries to rouse the constable, but, when he finally does so the 'ride' has passed by and all the rustics declare they know nothing about it. In Peter's Finger, the public house where the skimmington has been planned, all is quiet and innocent.

CHAPTER XL, *pp. 358–64*

Henchard witnesses the skimmington and then goes to see Elizabeth-Jane. He is told she is with Lucetta. He tries to inform the servants that Farfrae has been diverted to Mellstock but no one believes him. In his remorse, Henchard decides to go after Farfrae himself and tell him of his wife's plight. We see here the depths of human concern of which Henchard is capable even in defeat. He catches up with Farfrae and tries to persuade him of the seriousness of the situation and to make him return to Casterbridge. Farfrae, of course, does not believe him. He thinks that Henchard still wishes to kill him and refuses to turn back. The tragedy and irony of this are not lost on Henchard (p. 360).

Lucetta is now in great danger but there is nothing more Henchard can do. He goes home, the great thing in his heart now being his new regard for Elizabeth-Jane. Now he can at last appreciate her goodness, her human concern. Once home, he is told by Jopp that he has a visitor, a 'sea-captain of some sort'. Although we are not told, the man, of course, is Newson. He has come to reclaim his true daughter, Elizabeth-Jane, just as Henchard is coming truly to appreciate her worth.

The dying Lucetta tells Farfrae something of her relations with Henchard. Hardy does not make clear how much (p. 363).

Henchard, lingering around the house to see Elizabeth-Jane, is eventually told that Lucetta is dead. The humiliation of the skimmington had so upset her that, added to the weakness caused by her pregnancy, it has killed her.

CHAPTER XLI, *pp. 365–74*

Elizabeth-Jane comes to tell Henchard of Lucetta's death. Hardy makes clear Henchard's growing affection for the young woman. He no sooner does so than Newson knocks on the door. He explains his presence by telling his story. He recounts the tale of his 'marriage' to Susan and how, when the strains of that were becoming too great, he faked the news of his death (p. 367). He has come now to collect his daughter.

Henchard pretends that Elizabeth-Jane is dead and Newson departs. For the moment it is as simple as that. The effect on Henchard is to heighten even more his love for his 'daughter' (p. 368).

Henchard watches Newson go. Suddenly he is concerned that his fellow passengers will tell the man the truth. His worry again increases his affection for the girl. The description of his breakfast with her is delightful until Henchard feels obliged to tell her the truth about her parentage. He does not do this, however. Instead we are shown his suffering, above all his sense of tragic loss and isolation. It is in this mood that he wanders away contemplating suicide.

He is saved in the most bizarre way. He sees what appears to be his own body already floating in the water; it is, in fact, his effigy from the skimmington-ride. He returns home to be comforted by Elizabeth-Jane. He feels that he has to take her to the weir where she does indeed confirm what he has seen. Deeply moved by what she now understands as the depth of Henchard's desolation, Elizabeth-Jane begs to be allowed to live with him and comfort him. The moment is touchingly sincere. For some little while even Henchard can believe he is in the hands of a benevolent, superior power.

CHAPTER XLII, *pp. 375–82*

The feeling of security is destroyed by Henchard's worries over Newson, despite the fact that he seems to have gone for good.

Farfrae, ever a calculating man, decides not to revenge himself on the leaders of the skimmington (p. 375). But he fairly quickly gets over Lucetta's death which tells us a great deal about Farfrae's true nature. Indeed, Hardy's comments (p. 377) are vital to understanding the nature of his character.

Henchard now accepts the Council's gift of the little seed shop. Here he works quietly with Elizabeth-Jane, worrying nonetheless about Newson. Elizabeth-Jane, meanwhile, is being courted by Farfrae. Hardy introduces this subtly (p. 377). We see what Farfrae has been buying for the girl.

Eventually the truth about the relationship dawns on Henchard (p. 379), but he has lost much of his fighting spirit and does not seek to oppose the two. Nonetheless, their affair causes him much anguish (p. 380). He appreciates the dreadful irony that Farfrae is probably going to take from him the last thing in the world that is left to him. Despite the fact that the affair has not yet gone as far as a proposal, Henchard is well aware of the utter loneliness he would be plunged into if they were to marry. He refuses to submit to the temptation of telling Farfrae the truth of Elizabeth-Jane's birth.

CHAPTER XLIII, *pp. 383–92*

Elizabeth-Jane's affair with Farfrae becomes the common gossip. The rustics, it appears, are deeply sympathetic (p. 383).

Henchard, meanwhile, is becoming more and more withdrawn and 'morbidly sensitive'. He goes out and expects to spy on the young couple. The man he eventually sees is Newson. Henchard is terrified that he will tell Elizabeth-Jane the truth. When he returns home he discovers that Elizabeth-Jane has received an anonymous letter. He realizes now that revelation is certain and Hardy comments he 'was not the man to stand the certainty of condemnation on a matter so near his heart'. He would prefer to leave Casterbridge rather than be so humiliated and he tells Elizabeth-Jane that he is going. She is hurt, thinking his behaviour must be a reaction to her courtship. Of course, she does not understand the full and real reasons for Henchard's melancholy state.

Henchard dresses himself as a hay-trusser and leaves Casterbridge. The reversal of his fortunes is complete (p. 388). He accepts this with moving, stoic bravery.

Elizabeth-Jane, having accompanied her father some of his way, returns to Casterbridge where Farfrae introduces her to Newson. The true state of affairs is quickly revealed and as quickly accepted (p. 389). Arrangements for the marriage are made, not without some humour. As Newson explains how he saw through Henchard's lie about Elizabeth-Jane we see his own broadmindedness but also the horror, particularly in the eyes of Elizabeth-Jane, of what Henchard has done.

CHAPTER XLIV, *pp. 393–403*

Exhausted, Henchard falls asleep in an open field. In the morning he makes his way to Weydon-Priors. There is no fair here now but the place is charged with memories. Henchard makes his way to where, quite wrongly, he supposes the furmity tent to have stood. He is bitter, cheated and foiled. Only his love for Elizabeth-Jane still means anything to him. It is because of it that he cannot bring himself to leave the area and, despite realizing his foolishness, settles around Casterbridge (p. 395). He is back where he started out, but he has no energy left to try and rise again. Fate, the Gods, have seen to that.

Henchard is desperate for news of his 'daughter', desperate indeed to make contact with her (p. 397). He resolves to go to Casterbridge for the wedding day. He makes his way back, buying a caged goldfinch as a wedding present. By night, he creeps into the town and peers in at Farfrae's and Elizabeth-Jane's party (p. 400). The effect is one of the deepest pathos: the broken man watching a happiness he cannot share in a house where he is not welcome. The pain is made worse by Newson's clear acceptance here as the new and proper father of the couple.

When Henchard meets Elizabeth-Jane it is clear that she is bitter about his deception. Henchard slips away, defeated.

CHAPTER XLV, *pp. 404–11*

Having found his daughter and, without consciously doing so, wrecked Henchard's last chance of happiness, Newson moves to Budmouth to be nearer the sea. Elizabeth-Jane is brought the goldfinch her father bought her as a wedding present; abandoned on the night of the party, it has died from starvation. She knows intuitively who gave it to her and her feelings towards Henchard soften. She knows that he is the type of man who will 'live on as one of his own worst accusers'. She begs Farfrae to help her find him and they set out to do so.

They find Abel Whittle living in abject poverty. He has looked after Henchard because Henchard had been kind to his mother if cruel to him. His description of how he wished himself on to Henchard is moving, but Henchard himself has been dead for half an hour. The only human contact left with him is his will, his instructions that he be buried without mourners in unhallowed ground and that 'no man remember me'. It is Elizabeth-Jane who expresses the truth: 'what bitterness lies there!'

Henchard's last wishes are respected. His tragedy is over. We are left with Hardy's final view of Elizabeth-Jane as a modest, mature woman, stoical and wise in the knowledge that 'happiness was but the occasional episode in a general drama of pain'.

Characters

MICHAEL HENCHARD

Henchard is the true hero of *The Mayor of Casterbridge*, the true hero not simply because he is the major character but because he lives with that energy and passion we expect from the larger-than-life figures of legend. That Henchard is also the tragic hero, the victim of ill Fate and the flaws of his personality, gives him yet greater status. As Henchard moves through the novel we may sometimes despise him and at other times admire him, but, from fairly early on, we feel a pity which by the end is changed to awe at the sight of so massive a figure so wholly destroyed. It is precisely these feelings of pity and awe in the face of a great man's death that the writers of Greek tragedy were concerned to prompt. It is the effect Hardy achieves, too.

It is right that this mighty man should be built on a heroic scale. At the start we are told 'he was a fine figure, swarthy' and that his wife's shoulders were no higher than his elbow. Before his fight with Farfrae we see that he recognizes his superior physical powers (p. 344), while, when he saves Lucetta and Elizabeth-Jane from the bull, his sheer strength is made abundantly clear (pp. 278–80). Throughout, Hardy emphasizes the physical activity of the man. He is always on the move: walking, storming through his offices, running after people. When he is financially ruined it is certainly humiliating for him to go back to being a hay-trusser but the job is well within his physical capabilities.

Perhaps the most important physical description of Henchard comes in Chapter V. We see Henchard in triumph (p. 100). Hardy describes him as being 'of heavy frame', 'rather coarse than compact'. He is swarthy and has flashing black eyes. He has a large mouth, fine teeth and a harsh laugh. Hardy elaborates on this laugh: 'Its producer's personal goodness, if he had any, would be of a very fitful caste – an occasional almost oppressive generosity rather than a mild and constant kindness.' This is no orderly creature of quiet moral virtue. Henchard is a man whose huge stature reveals a volatile temper. Henchard is indeed a man of moods. He is impulsive, easily angered and sometimes cruel. He is also a passionate man of robust intelligence and strong emotions. He can be generous, compassionate, even sentimental. He can also be cruel and a bully. Finally, he is a man terribly alone. Such energies as these can raise him from being a peasant labourer to a figure of power. They can also drag him down below the level at which he started. Just as he is introduced to us as a nameless peasant so Henchard, having risen and fallen, will beg to be buried in a nameless grave.

The most striking characteristics of Henchard are his energy and impulsiveness. At the start of the book we see a young and embittered man whose energy has been sapped by a loveless marriage. We see his cruelty and impulsiveness when he auctions off his wife. The following morning Henchard is a remorseful man, but the next time we see him he is in triumph. His energies have been released and used. He is rich and successful, the mayor of Casterbridge.

Such violent changes are characteristic. We see them most crucially in Henchard's relations with Farfrae. To be sure, the young Scot has the means of saving Henchard from great embarrassment, but Henchard takes to him with 'tigerish affection'. He invites the man who is to work his destruction into his home, considers giving him a third of his wealth and treats him with breezy familiarity. After his reunion with Susan, Henchard opens up his deeper feelings to him. We see the melancholy side of this open-hearted man. We see his loneliness when he feels that the world has 'the blackness of hell'. We see in his revelations about Lucetta the impulsive way he goes about satisfying his deep need for affection.

Such energies can build up a mighty business from nothing but they are not – and Henchard knows this – able to maintain order and system. When Henchard returns from his dramatic reunion with Susan (Chapter XII) he finds Farfrae going over the accounts. Henchard knows that he himself is 'mentally and physically unfit for grubbing subtleties from soiled paper' and he knows that he needs the calculating Farfrae. Indeed, he has been looking for such a complement to his own intense personality for some two years. He has run his business by 'rule o' thumb', by the rough-and-ready methods one might expect from such a man. His intelligence and industry, his huge personality and good luck have made him fortunate. When misfortune such as the 'growed wheat' comes his way he tends to shrug it off, taking the rough with the smooth.

Henchard has, however, a deep sense of responsibility towards other people. He can be sharp, even brutal. The selling of his wife is callous; he can hurt Elizabeth-Jane deeply; when cornered by the threat of bankruptcy he can blackmail Lucetta into a promise of marriage. But he also possesses a deep and growing regard for others. Part of this stems from duty, part of it, especially as regards Elizabeth-Jane, flows from an increasing greatness and delicacy of heart. Henchard is a fundamentally moral man. Despite overflowing feelings he knows what is proper, as we see in his steeling himself to 'remarry' Susan; equally, when he is offered opportunities to revenge himself on Lucetta and Farfrae, he turns them down.

Henchard married Susan when he was little more than a boy. The man, we feel, is far too passionate to be tied to her. However, Henchard has done Susan wrong, he knows he has done her wrong, and he is determined to make amends, to provide for his 'daughter' and to 'castigate' himself by lowering his dignity and 'marrying' a humble woman (p. 154). Henchard has a firm grip on right and wrong. He will deny himself to see that right is done and he has the will-power to follow this through. It is precisely this that turns the pathos of Elizabeth-Jane being Newson's child into tragic irony.

Again, although he describes himself as being something of a 'woman-hater', Henchard needs women's love and he is not prepared to abuse it. He is determined to act honourably towards Lucetta and when this is no longer necessary it is tragic that she reveals herself as fickle. She excites the man and then turns to Farfrae. Henchard's frustration and bitterness are natural. His attempt to blackmail her into marriage reveals again the cruelty that goes with Henchard's impulsive nature but his betrayal is really far worse a thing.

Lucetta is finally married to Farfrae because she cannot bring herself to marry Henchard after the furmity-woman's revelations. It is at this point in the novel, two-thirds of the way through, that we see most clearly a further component that is essential to understanding Henchard's character: the fact that he is the victim of Fate.

We have seen his treatment of Susan and how he has tried to make amends. We have seen how desperately he wants to love Elizabeth-Jane and how betrayed he feels when he discovers she is not his daughter. We have seen Lucetta's worth and how he has treated her. We have watched all this and felt that Henchard is neither completely innocent nor completely guilty. In addition we have been shown how Henchard's affection for Farfrae has turned to deep-seated jealousy, how Henchard has hurried on a clash of irreconcilable personalities. All of these things now gather to work his destruction. Henchard has done right by Susan but the furmity-woman's revelations destroy Henchard socially. Through the sheer malevolence of Nature Henchard has been financially ruined. Lucetta has obliterated his hopes of love. Henchard is very far from being simply a good man but he is now to be punished out of all proportion to his wickedness.

Henchard shows dignity at the bankruptcy proceedings and greatness of heart after them. He sells his gold watch to pay off a creditor who would otherwise have been ruined. He humbles himself sufficiently to work for Farfrae. When his new master offers him rooms in his own home and even the return of some of his furniture, Henchard is too proud to take them. But just as his rise to wealth showed the complexity of his personality, so his fall shows that he is neither perfectly good nor wholly capable of being mean and vengeful. To be sure, Henchard starts drinking again and, when drunk, can show his spite towards Farfrae and Lucetta. Nonetheless, when he has the chance of humiliating Lucetta and revealing her past to Farfrae he cannot do it. We know that he is both a strong and a violent man. We have seen this in the fight he has with Farfrae. We see also here that he believes strongly in fair play and, when given the chance to kill the man who has replaced him, he spurns it. Again, he does not finally betray Lucetta. As Hardy comments: 'Such a wrecking of hearts appalled even him. His quality was such that he could have annihilated them both in the heat of action, but to accomplish the deed by oral poison was beyond the nerve of his enmity.' Instead, when Lucetta has been made fatally ill by the skimmington-ride Henchard chases after Farfrae to tell him how badly his wife needs him. Despite his humiliation on the occasion of the royal visit (a humiliation which Henchard in his pathetic obstinacy deserves) he tries to save the life and marriage of the woman who has betrayed him. This shows altruism of a high order. Henchard's impulsiveness does not always work harm. In the largeness of his heart he strives to forgive and help his enemy. That he is rebuffed is yet a further tragic irony.

Another indication of Henchard's growing stature in defeat is his treatment of Elizabeth-Jane. From the moment of their introduction he had wanted to love her and strong paternal feelings are at work within him. When the truth of Elizabeth-Jane's paternity is revealed Henchard is cold and harsh, but, as he sinks further and further and Elizabeth-Jane's deep reserves of human sympathy become ever clearer, so Henchard begins to value her as a woman in her own right. Quietly and unpretentiously she comes to live with him and look after him. He learns to love in a strong and grateful way. We come to see that she is his own defence against the utter loneliness that Henchard fears perhaps above all else. He becomes gentle towards her and (we cannot blame him) lies to keep her close to him. This is the desperate gesture of a man who knows the true horror of loneliness. Of course, it fails. That Henchard suffers because of his lie shows he still preserves his strong sense of right and wrong, but that Elizabeth-Jane is finally taken from him by her true father and by Farfrae is perhaps the cruellest irony of all. It adds tremendous pathos to the closing chapters that Henchard is deprived of the one person that he truly loves.

Henchard goes away because he is not wanted; he is an intruder on the happiness of others. They reject him because of his deceit. In their own terms, Elizabeth-Jane, Farfrae and Newson are right. That we know how greatly Henchard is suffering removes from us any wish to blame him for what he has done. In his final broken state, abandoned, impoverished and cast out, a most delicate poetry and love is aroused within him. Henchard resolves to wander far away with only a few mementoes of Elizabeth-Jane to treasure. But he cannot do so. His heart is fixed in a place where it is not wanted, is rejected and despised. Henchard realizes this and the pathos of it all is the more profound for his realization (p. 395).

He secretly watches the wedding party of Farfrae and Elizabeth-Jane. The sense of defeat and exclusion, the picture of the broken man with his unwanted wedding present staring in at the celebrations, are almost unbearable. Pity and awe – the true effects of tragedy – are indeed summoned as we see the broken hero wander away to die and beg for burial in an anonymous grave.

DONALD FARFRAE

Farfrae is conceived as Henchard's opposite. Where Henchard is impulsive, passionate and finally defeated, Farfrae is calculating, cool and ultimately successful. Where Henchard represents the old ways of agriculture, the 'rule o' thumb' approach, Farfrae is the young, modern man of science. He stands for progress. In the end, he stands for success. He completely replaces Henchard. He takes from the older man first his mistress and then his daughter, he buys out his bankrupt business and becomes himself the mayor of Casterbridge.

Hardy's portrayal of Farfrae is subtle. Although Farfrae wins on the material level, there is no question but that he is a lesser man than Henchard. He is younger, slighter and emotionally much shallower. He is mean with his money and almost continuously self-satisfied. However, if we cannot wholly like him, neither can we utterly despise him. Farfrae can be kind, he is fair and he is honest. He usually acts for the best as he sees it. His failure, when we measure him against Henchard, is essentially a failure of imagination. Put simply, Farfrae has very little insight into human suffering – and human suffering is what the novel is all about.

Farfrae is introduced to us as the young, ambitious, scientific farmer about to set off for America. In the event, he brings the New World to Casterbridge. He hears of the 'growed wheat', and with no thought to his own profit sends Henchard a note telling him he can help him. He shows Henchard the device and the older man is stunned by what seems to him to be almost magic. Eventually, after very considerable persuasion from Henchard, he agrees to stay in Casterbridge where he establishes himself as the modern, efficient new man whom Henchard realizes he needs. Farfrae can keep accounts, run a business well and proves popular with the workforce. Indeed, this is part of Henchard's undoing. Good labour relations are part of Farfrae's modern approach. Where Henchard rules by fear and blustering, Farfrae stands for sensible decency. When Abel Whittle is humiliated by Henchard (pp. 169–70) Farfrae will have nothing to do with it. He even threatens to resign. This is not the act of a cold, calculating man. Such moves as this establish Farfrae in the people's hearts. His songs have already won them over. Now they begin to rely on his judgement. They prefer him to Henchard when they want their haystacks valued. When a celebration is thrown they prefer to attend Farfrae's, even though they have to pay an entrance fee. Farfrae's music and dancing, his lighthearted youth and energy appeal far more than Henchard's stormy largesse. It is when Henchard comes to Farfrae's entertainment that he discovers how he is being replaced in the people's affections and dismisses the man who was once his friend.

When Farfrae sets up in business on his own he is scrupulously fair to the man who had once been so kind to him. While Henchard vows fairly but utterly to annihilate Farfrae, the young Scot merely sees this competition in terms of fair and honest business. But Farfrae is also both lucky and an innovator. It is he who introduces the seed-drill to Casterbridge, the instrument of the new technology that makes sure nothing is wasted. It is he who speculates successfully on the harvest. There is no emotion for him in all of this and when Henchard is finally bankrupt Farfrae cannot understand the depth of the older man's anger. He exposes his naïvety in a significant speech (p. 315).

It is Elizabeth-Jane who points out (p. 240) what emotional loss such methods as Farfrae's bring, but, while Farfrae recognizes this, he bows before his own God: progress. The rustics who loved him may come to envy him for his success, but even when he cuts their pay they are willing to work for him. Farfrae's modern technology may be somewhat bloodless, but at least it provides regular work and order, a welcome release from the stormy and ultimately inefficient Henchard (p. 295).

Henchard takes to Farfrae with 'tigerish affection'. There is little evidence that any warmth of friendship is returned beyond decent gratitude. Farfrae does not see the need for anything more and, while this is prudent, it is far from exciting. Indeed, it appears to make him seem rather shallow. Farfrae is unable to appreciate the depth of Henchard's melancholy (p. 149) and is relatively unmoved by his bizarre past and later 'remarriage' (p. 154). A certain mild curiosity is all he is prepared to show and probably all he feels. When he sets up in competition with Henchard, Farfrae has a young man's sense of fair play. There is nothing of blood and thunder in his approach and he is undeniably successful. He takes calculated risks as every businessman does (p. 231). Unlike Henchard, for Farfrae these are merely part of his job. That he is successful is not a cause for triumph, though the scene of his first meeting with Lucetta (chapter XXIII) certainly reveals that success has made him smug. That the woman can drive him to a spontaneous gesture of kindness clearly makes him a little uncomfortable but it is not wholly out of character. We see later that, when pressed, Farfrae is prepared to help set his defeated rival up in a small business. Certainly he feels sufficiently sorry for Henchard to offer him rooms in his old house and even the return of some of his furniture. No doubt he thinks he is being rather magnanimous. There can be little question however that he is also somewhat unimaginative. It shows a very limited understanding of Henchard's pride that Farfrae believes he might accept such offers. Again, there is lack of imagination (although this time we cannot blame him) when he refuses to return to Casterbridge with Henchard when he is told of Lucetta's illness. The great fight has just taken place between the two men and Farfrae is understandably suspicious of Henchard. The older man himself has made a heroic effort to do good to his rival. It is, to be sure, an effort he makes in vain, but we can hardly blame Farfrae for misunderstanding him. After all, he has failed to understand the depths of the man's emotions all the way through.

This failure of imagination is starkest when Farfrae and Elizabeth-Jane go out in search of the defeated Henchard in the last chapters. Farfrae, we feel, is acting very much out of a sense of duty towards a man to whom he owes no real obligation. He resents the cost of the expedition and it is Elizabeth-Jane, not he, who appreciates the depth of bitterness in Henchard's last will.

Much of Farfrae's shallowness is revealed in his dealings with women. Indeed, at one point, Hardy tells us pointedly that: 'the fact was that he knew very little of sex'. He also tells us (p. 245) that compared to Farfrae, Henchard was 'like the sun beside the moon'. Farfrae is not indifferent to women: when thrown together with Elizabeth-Jane he clearly enjoys their little, lighthearted erotic scene, but he is also well aware that the girl's simple modesty and powerful father would make her a useful wife. When the relationship is no longer prudent, however, Farfrae is perfectly capable of letting it go. It is clear also that he is attracted to Lucetta, but the attentive reader must decide how far she is responsible for leading him on. Certainly, she enjoys arousing him and lets herself be involved as far as her own somewhat facile emotions will allow her to be. However, while Farfrae is a dutiful and, in his way, loving husband, the shallowness of his emotions is brutally revealed after Lucetta's death (p. 377). There is not to be any prolonged mourning by Farfrae. Just as, when he first met Lucetta, half his heart was set on getting back to the market-place, so after her death his 'brisk' nature takes him back there. Certainly he does not love so deeply as to follow through his revenge on the organizers of the skimmington. The idea passes through his mind but he dismisses it as being unwise. Like everything else, Farfrae's emotions are judged by the ultimate criteria of profit and loss.

Finally, Farfrae marries Elizabeth-Jane. There is a conventional charm about their courtship. Farfrae buys her presents, they meet secretly, they become engaged and Henchard's exclusion from their happiness breaks his heart. This has relatively little effect on Farfrae.

He has found the loyal, demure wife he needs. Certainly it is not his love for Elizabeth-Jane that sustains her as we see her at the close. Her marriage to Farfrae brings her social prestige and for that she is relatively grateful. But there is no feeling of great love. Elizabeth-Jane is at peace with the world because she has come to look on it with philosophically-lowered eyes; they are certainly not eyes lit by love for her husband.

In sum, Farfrae is a modern, scientific man, a believer in progress and success. He is rational, decent and unflamboyant. He acts decently where he can and is almost invariably in control of what emotions he has. He is human but calculating. He ends the novel rich, successful but cut off from that tragic vision of life which may be horribly destructive, even self-destructive, but is nonetheless far more enriching than the life of a man who can grub 'subtleties from soiled paper'.

ELIZABETH-JANE

Hardy ends the novel with a portrait of Elizabeth-Jane. She is now a mature, married woman. She is philosophical and accepting, a stoic who has learned the art of 'making limited opportunities endurable'. To be sure, she has acquired some social status, but Elizabeth-Jane does not let herself be carried away by this. She has been schooled by chance and suffering and she is now too wise to look on the world with enthusiasm. This is the final wisdom Hardy wishes to leave us.

The ending is important. We see at last a woman who is stable, sure of what she is and where she stands. This has been far from the case throughout most of the novel. Indeed, confusion about who Elizabeth-Jane is is central to Hardy's effects. For a long time Henchard and most readers assume she is the baby we see at the start grown up. When we discover this is not so Elizabeth-Jane herself has come to believe that she is Henchard's daughter. The final catastrophe is precipitated when the young woman discovers that her real father is Newson.

Why does Hardy surround Elizabeth-Jane with so much confusion about her identity? Partly, of course, it is pure entertainment, the pleasure we get from constant reversals and surprises. Part of it comes unavoidably from the development of the plot. But there are two other reasons: it is through such confusions and misunderstandings that Hardy shows us the sheer cruel irony of Fate; secondly, when at the end of the novel Elizabeth-Jane is sure who she is and where she belongs, we feel that she has richly experienced life and that the conclusions she has come to are the fruits of that experience. Because we have watched her struggle, seen her accepted and reviled, we trust her final conclusions (end of chapter XLV, p. 411). Elizabeth-Jane, after all, has earned the right to think like this.

The confusion about who she is makes Elizabeth-Jane the innocent victim of chance and irony. As such, she is as central to the themes of the book as Henchard himself. Like him, too, she is often lonely. But her loneliness does not make her bitter, nor, unlike Henchard, does it make her throw herself into extreme situations. She does not elope nor make grand gestures. Instead, she sits still, suffers and watches. Hardy describes her as 'a spectator of all that went on without herself being particularly seen'. Again, perhaps rather cruelly, she is called a 'dumb deep-feeling, great-eyed creature'. Lucetta describes her as lonely (p. 287).

As she watches, Elizabeth-Jane learns wisdom. It is she who spies the growing rift between Henchard and Farfrae, and it is through her eyes that we see it. It is she who knows that Jopp is the wrong man for Henchard to employ. It is she who sees the absurdity of Henchard's and Farfrae's vying for Lucetta. As she watches and suffers, Elizabeth-Jane learns:

... the lesson of renunciation, and was as familiar with the wreck of each day's wishes as with the diurnal setting of the sun.

It is this girl who grows into the woman we see at the close.

Suffering can make people hard, even heartless, and this Elizabeth-Jane is not. She can inspire love of a sort in Farfrae and the description of her learning to dress herself attractively (p. 166) and then being mildly embarrassed by the result has great charm. The meeting with Farfrae which her mother engineers (chapter XIV) shows that she is not averse to pleasure. There are two further characteristics which are of great importance: Elizabeth-Jane's innate kindliness and her very strong sense of duty, her passion for discerning right and wrong. Of her kindness Hardy writes (near the beginning of the chapter, p. 112):

> If there was one good thing more than another which characterized this single-hearted girl it was a willingness to sacrifice her personal comfort and dignity to the common weal.

She is kind to servants (p. 201) and thinks nothing of waitressing in the Three Mariners to provide for her mother. But her sheer, strong, spontaneous kindness is shown in her treatment of Henchard. For all that he bullies and cajoles her, she cannot let him suffer alone. As he falls, so her generosity towards him becomes greater. She nurses him, protects him and, perhaps most important of all, stays by him during much of his growing loneliness. Despite everything, she earns his love and this Henchard is terrified of losing. Indeed, it is precisely the depth of his love for this good creature who is not his daughter and whom he has so abused, that gives truly tragic pathos to Henchard's last days.

But he lies for her sake. He convinces Newson that Elizabeth-Jane is dead. The reader can only be sympathetic to this. We know how desperately Henchard needs Elizabeth-Jane. What we also know is Elizabeth-Jane's absolute and clear-cut belief in right and wrong. When she is told of Lucetta's marriage to Farfrae she leaves High-Place Hall without a second thought (p. 290). Indeed, this whole section of the novel shows her rigorous principles, and we see that these too are a response to early suffering (near the end of the chapter, p. 289):

> Any suspicion of impropriety was to Elizabeth-Jane like a red rag to a bull. Her craving for correctness of procedure was, indeed, almost vicious.

It is because of this that she rejects Henchard so utterly when she learns that Newson is indeed her true father. To us, this may seem rather absolute, even priggish. To Hardy's contemporary readers it would have seemed less so. Elizabeth-Jane does the right thing. It results in her final cold parting with Henchard, but as she recognizes the bitterness with which Henchard penned his will we see that she still has depths of feeling, feeling which experience teaches her to keep well in check.

LUCETTA

Lucetta is a stock Victorian character – the lady 'with a past'. And she suddenly makes her appearance from that past to disturb the present. She was the daughter of a military officer and lived in the Channel Islands. Henchard had met her there when he was on a business-trip and they had fallen in love. Their liaison would have been seen as contrary to Victorian moral standards and that fact itself would encourage secrecy.

It is interesting to note that Lucetta's need for secrecy was shared by Henchard. But, whilst Lucetta thought their secret was safe from the world, she also thought that they had no secrets between them. According to a letter which arrives in Casterbridge soon after Henchard's 're-marriage' to Susan, he had appeared to be frank with Lucetta. He had told her of his separation from his wife and that he had not heard from her for 'fifteen or sixteen years'. Henchard had obviously not told her the whole truth. We know that the selling of his wife came as a complete shock to Lucetta. The news first came to her when it exploded in Casterbridge after the notorious court case involving the old furmity-woman (chapter XXVIII). It is Lucetta who charges him with selling Susan 'like a horse or a cow' (p. 284).

This awareness of the need for secrecy is something which will torment Lucetta throughout her short married life to Farfrae. She is always afraid that her earlier relationship with Henchard will somehow come to light. Ironically, she has provided the very means of her own destruction. Hardy tells us that 'Lucetta was rather addicted to scribbling' (p. 220) and it was this need to pen her thoughts that was to cause her such distress. She had written passionate love letters to Henchard, and the first thing we hear from her in the novel is through the medium of a letter. In a fittingly ironic touch from Hardy, the letter is requesting the return of other letters. Those letters are used against her and, indirectly, cause her death.

Such a constant and frequent appeal for the letters is a sign that Lucetta is not a trusting kind of woman. She certainly does not trust Henchard. We may feel, from the scene where he reads parts of the letters to Farfrae, that she had grounds for such mistrust. It might be more accurate to suggest that her willingness to attribute such motives and actions to Henchard stems from her own facility in using people to her own advantage.

Her first action on arriving at Casterbridge is underhand and devious. She takes advantage of the misery of another woman. She persuades Elizabeth-Jane to come and live with her at High-Place Hall and appears to be doing Elizabeth-Jane a favour. In reality she is only thinking of herself. In a note to Henchard she speaks condescendingly about Elizabeth-Jane and tells him that she has invited her to stay at High-Place Hall 'to give you an excuse for coming here as if to visit *her*' (p. 220). Henchard sums up our feelings when he speaks of Lucetta as an 'artful little woman'. That might sound approving but a little later he gives expression to another sentiment in regard to Lucetta as representing all women: 'there's not an inch of straight grain in 'em' (p. 221). Certainly she proves this most cruelly to Henchard later in the novel. She complains at one point that Henchard had placed her in a 'dilemma' in Jersey. It can have been only slight by comparison with the dilemmas he provides for her in Casterbridge. We have to sympathize with her somewhat. But, being a resourceful woman, she quickly solves her problem by first promising to marry Henchard and then immediately leaving Casterbridge to marry Donald Farfrae at Port-Bredy. The affair with Farfrae was itself a display of strategy on her part. Again she uses Elizabeth-Jane to justify his visits to High-Place Hall. In the public's mind he was visiting both ladies there. In reality both he and Lucetta ignored Elizabeth-Jane in the most highhanded fashion. One might excuse this in Lucetta on the grounds that she was a woman in love, but we have too much evidence of her designing ways to be too generous towards her. We remember the wily ways in which she prepared herself for that first intended visit of Henchard to High-Place Hall, where she 'arranged herself picturesquely' (p. 227).

In sum, Lucetta is a frivolous and pathetic creature aware of her power over men but unwilling to accept responsibility for the consequences. She looks lightly on life, acts on impulse and suffers for it. She dies, literally, of shame.

SUSAN HENCHARD

Susan is not simply the grey, indeterminate figure that the people of Casterbridge see. They obviously view her as a thoroughly ordinary woman. They express considerable surprise, for example, at her ever having the opportunity to marry their mayor, Michael Henchard. One spectator at the wedding describes her as 'a poor twanking woman' with 'hardly a pair of jumps or nightrail to her name' (p. 156). In these dialect terms she is thus summed up as mournful and impoverished. Her good fortune in being able to make such a fine catch as Michael Henchard is seen as highly ironic by the rustics. The irony is that it is not a love-match at all but a marriage of convenience. Henchard has 'married' her to help salve his conscience. She has married Henchard to correct what she regards as a misdemeanour committed nineteen years before.

We have to travel back those nineteen years to begin an effective study of Susan. She appears so briefly in our first meeting with her that we might tend to ignore her. We might have failed to notice that this young woman had more than a touch of beauty. The beauty lay in the 'mobility', as Hardy calls it, of her face. The word suggests a lively intelligence, a promise, perhaps, of spirit. The possibility of passion is caught in Hardy's description of how the sun 'set fire on her lips' (p. 70). We see a flash of that spirit in her reaction to the appalling behaviour of her young husband in selling her. She 'flung' her wedding ring into his face. In addition to that it is she who seems to make the first move away from Henchard, for we see her 'seizing the sailor's arm with her right hand' and leading him out of the tent.

So, certainly when young, she had her pride and her sense of independence. Hardy tones this effect down somewhat in the opening chapter by stating that, despite her expression of will, she is a victim of those twin forces of Time and Chance that bedevil the lives of the leading personalities in this novel. She is part of the pessimistic landscape of the book, for the last thing she expects from life is 'fair play' (p. 70). By singling out this fatalistic perspective in relation to Susan, Hardy does lend her significance in the novel. We are led to feel that we ought not to underrate Susan. Being one who would not expect 'fair play' to be part of existence, she may well not see the point of indulging in it herself.

So it is that we find Susan Henchard deliberately hiding from Michael the whole truth of those nineteen years. The identity of Elizabeth-Jane is kept away from him while she is alive. The truth explodes on him after her death and destroys an affection that was beginning to flower. This deception affects the reader's relationship with Susan Henchard too. For, like Michael, we are duped. The author is working with his character here in deceiving the reader and we are thus helped to appreciate Henchard's feelings when he discovers the truth.

Thus, while Susan is dull on the surface, she has determination and a dangerous naïve cunning. She tricks Farfrae and Elizabeth-Jane into meeting and eventually they marry. She deceives Henchard into thinking Elizabeth-Jane is his daughter. We cannot call Susan evil – far from it – but we can see her as a remorseless instrument of revenge. She is too simple a soul to realize that she is this; nonetheless, it is her return, her plotting, that ensure Henchard's downfall.

THE RUSTICS

In another section of this book, we examine *The Mayor of Casterbridge* as tragedy (pp. 83–5). Reference is made there to the Greek ideas about what elements tragedy contains. One significant element that is omitted there for inclusion here is that of the chorus.

In Greek tragedy, the chorus was seen as a commentary on the action. The choral group would reflect on the significance of various actions, on the part played by fate, on the human condition, and such large issues. We see this kind of thing happening through the various members of Hardy's 'chorus' – the rustic group. Unlike the Greek chorus, they are not anonymous: we know them as Christopher Coney, Buzzford, Solomon Longways, Mother Cuxsom, Nance Mockridge. Unlike the Greek chorus, too, they do not chant in unison, but offer their commentary as individuals, though, in another sense, they all speak with one voice.

After Susan's death Mother Cuxsom makes a moving commentary on the way worldly realities pass away and become insignificant. The secrets Susan kept so carefully will be exposed to view since 'all her shining keys will be took from her' (p. 191). There is a pessimistic ring about these sentiments that echoes their comments on the occasion of Susan's wedding. The rustics assume the role of prophets of doom, anticipating the worst for Susan Henchard and, at the same time, forecasting a troubled relationship between her and Michael. Nance Mockridge expresses the view (end of the chapter, p. 156) that:

She'll wish her cake dough afore she's done of him. There's a bluebeardy look about 'em; and 'twill out in time.

The rustic chorus also performs the function of providing some background information at times and thus offers some variety in Hardy's narrative style. So, it is through them that Susan learns of the importance of Michael Henchard in Casterbridge (chapter V). It is they, too, who help to create a picture of another side of Caster-bridge much contrasted with the apparently respectable middle-class commercial community. In chapter VIII they paint an unattractive picture of Casterbridge both past and present. It is a picture that leaps into life much later in the novel where the choric members take on another dimension as we see the cruelty of the skimmington-ride.

So far, we have seen them as a collective entity. Later they assume a more active part and more distinguishable separate traits. In accordance with Aristotle's theory of tragedy they 'assume a share in the action'. If we single out one of the choric characters for special attention, we can see that he actually undergoes a change of heart in the course of the tale.

When we first meet Christopher Coney he sounds cynical and seems to see the irony of things. He listens in the Three Mariners to Farfrae's songs of Scotland and expresses surprise that Farfrae could ever have left such a delightful place since he thinks so much about it. As he says to Farfrae: 'Be dazed, if I loved my country half as well as the young feller do, I'd live by claning my neighbour's pigsties afore I'd go away!' (p. 122). We can easily recognize the tone of these words and the suspicion he has of Farfrae's motives. Yet, later, when the skimmington-ride is being planned, it is Christopher Coney and Solomon Longways who devise a scheme to save Farfrae from the immediate impact of that event. Even then he is not fully persuaded that Farfrae is worthy of their protection, for he thinks of him as a man 'engrossed with affairs and ambitions'; but he still helps Solomon to save Farfrae from this 'rough joke'.

Hardy has shown us more than once that the rustics enjoy a coarse brand of humour. Though Elizabeth-Jane 'disliked those wretched humours of Christopher Coney and his tribe' they were not always so poisonous. They enjoy a particular brand of ribald humour and this is evident when they are talking about the marriage of Susan and Michael Henchard. Solomon Longways draws good-humoured attention to Mother Cuxsom's vast size when he asks how Susan, 'a mere skellinton', could have landed such a fine husband 'while a woman of your tonnage have not' (p. 155). A similar contrast can be drawn between these two on the occasion when the skimmington-ride is planned (chapter XXXVI). When Lucetta's correspondence comes to light Mother Cuxsom sees it as a chance for some innocent, if bawdy, fun. The skimmington is, however, Nance Mockridge's vindictive idea. She sees Lucetta's conduct as a reflection on themselves as 'respectable women'. She takes herself seriously where Mother Cuxsom has a developed sense of fun. It is typical of the novel that the tragic events prevail over this sense of fun.

Commentary

THE MAYOR OF CASTERBRIDGE AS TRAGEDY

In his *General Preface to the Wessex Edition of 1912* (reprinted in the Penguin edition of *The Mayor of Casterbridge*, pp. 413–18), Hardy refers to 'our magnificent heritage from the Greeks in dramatic Literature'. It is no surprise, then, that it should be so simple to trace the influence of Greek tragedy on his own telling of *The Mayor of Casterbridge*.

One of the great theorists of tragedy, Aristotle, talking of the central figure in a tragedy, specifies that 'the change in the hero's fortunes must not be from misery to happiness, but on the contrary from happiness to misery'. This is a blueprint for the depiction of Michael Henchard in *The Mayor of Casterbridge*. We find him in chapter V of the novel in a position of supreme authority in the town and obviously enjoying every minute of it. Forty chapters later he is a broken man who dies in poverty and as an outcast.

Aristotle had other things to say about characters and characterization. The most notable of his observations is that a tragic character should suffer 'not due to vice and depravity, but rather to some error'. This would tie in with Hardy's treatment of Henchard, for it could not be claimed that Henchard is an evil man. It could be claimed that he is a man who makes more than one serious error, errors which he almost immediately recognizes but finds are irrevocable. For example, he invites both Farfrae and Elizabeth-Jane, at separate times, to leave him completely. As soon as they have severed their connection, he wishes immediately to restore the relationships.

Aristotle also required that the tragic hero be a man in an exalted position. This would make his fall the more dramatic. Henchard, it is true, never loses his peasant nature, but in his role as mayor he is a figure of great power and prestige. His fall is the more moving for his being a self-made man.

Elsewhere in his account of characterization in tragedy, Aristotle points out that this ought always to be consistent. Hardy is at one with this opinion and stressed in his own writings that he would wish to avoid 'improbabilities of character'.

In addition to this emphasis on convincing characterization, the Greek theorist stressed the need for careful and convincing plot construction. He insists on the notion of unity of plot which he describes in this way: 'the plot of a play, being the representation of an action, must present it as a unified whole; and its various incidents must be so arranged that if any one of them is differently placed or taken away, the effect of the wholeness will be seriously disrupted'. He could well have been describing the plotting of *The Mayor of Casterbridge*, for it could be used persuasively as an exemplar of this interdependence of one action on another and the contribution of each separate part to the whole effect.

The depiction of character and the organization of plot may be seen as the mechanics of tragedy. But why do these have to be so perfect? Why does such care have to be taken in their construction? The answer is that the design of tragedy is to achieve the effects of 'pity and fear'. We have to be led to believe that what we witness could happen to us. We feel, to quote Aristotle, 'pity for the undeserving sufferer and fear for the man like ourselves'.

These emotions of pity and fear are not to be seen as unattractive. We are to feel some pleasure in them, and they are intended to have a positively beneficial effect on us. Aristotle talks of this as a 'catharsis'. This is a process which prepares us to deal with problems in our own lives through witnessing their presence in the lives of others. Elizabeth-Jane in *The Mayor of Casterbridge* is one who has benefited in this way. Hardy tells us that, having learned the lessons of pain, she was able, not only to enjoy existence but to teach others to deal with it more effectively. Hardy tells us this (p. 410) in what is an epilogue to his story. Such is the essential message of tragedy as the Greeks understood that form, and it is the central message of *The Mayor of Casterbridge*.

What has been outlined so far might be described as a 'purist' approach to tragedy. Hardy acknowledges throughout his novel the intrusion of external and powerful influences and Aristotle disapproved of this. The gods, the 'Powers' as Farfrae calls them, frequently assert themselves and exert their influence on man's fate. *The Mayor of Casterbridge* does not contain a specific statement about the 'Powers', but the pessimistic notion of Fate, circumstance and forces beyond our control, pervades the novel and lends it a further tragic dimension. These forces often reveal themselves through irony.

IRONY

You will find a great many references in these notes to irony in the novel. The reason is that it is one of the most pervasive features of Hardy's style. It is a device closely linked with the tragic impulse of the novel, and with the constant insistence by Hardy on the intrusive nature of Fate in man's affairs.

By irony we mean that an event occurs which in itself is either harmless or even desirable, but that it occurs, say, at an inappropriate time and has an opposite effect to that intended. This is to be attributed, in Hardy's novel, to the ill designs of Fate.

Perhaps the most cogent expression of despair at this state of affairs is uttered, uncharacteristically, by Farfrae. It occurs on an occasion where Lucetta appeals to him to leave Casterbridge. She feels threatened by Henchard, and especially by her fear that her past liaison with him will be revealed. Farfrae seems willing for them to leave, but at that very instant 'a visitor was announced' (p. 315). He brings the news that the mayor, Doctor Chalkfeld, has died, and that a vacancy has, therefore, occurred. The office of mayor is now offered to Farfrae. It seems a reasonable offer, a gift from the gods, as Farfrae expresses it (p. 316). The irony is that the timely opportunity seems like a blessing. It is to prove a curse.

Michael Henchard too is dogged by ironic twists of fortune. A full list of examples would be too long, but here a few of the more conspicuous will exemplify the issue effectively. The most powerful example of irony is that which occurs in chapter XIX. It is midway through the novel and corresponds to the highpoint of a Shakespearean tragedy where the hero experiences his greatest despair. In this case, Michael Henchard feels secure. He experiences a peace with Elizabeth-Jane that contrasts sharply with the troubles associated with Susan, her dead mother. Now, he feels, is the ideal time to reveal to her the reality as he understands it. In a poignant scene, he reveals the 'truth' of her origins to Elizabeth-Jane and pleads with her to accept that he is her father. The bitter irony of his timing explodes on him and the reader at that juncture. For, no sooner has he established this relationship, than he discovers the truth for himself. A letter from Susan informs him of the true identity of Elizabeth-Jane. Hardy refers to it as a 'blasting disclosure'.

Notes, letters, messages – all have a role to play in the ironic twists of fortune in the novel. One outstanding example of this is the note that throws Farfrae and Lucetta together. Henchard, realizing that he could rid himself of Elizabeth-Jane's company by inviting Farfrae to renew his romantic interest in her, writes a note to Farfrae (chapter XX). In the note, he points out that he does not wish 'to interfere with your courtship of Elizabeth-Jane'. The note does the trick. The irony is that, when Farfrae calls upon Elizabeth-Jane at High-Place Hall (chapter XXII), he meets not her but Lucetta. They fall in love. Lucetta looks particularly appealing at this point because she had been expecting Henchard to call on her in response to various notes from *her*. Part of the irony of the new relationship between Lucetta and Farfrae is that it has an equal and opposite result to that which Farfrae had hoped to achieve. He had seen his courtship of Elizabeth-Jane as providing 'a reconciliation with his former friend Henchard' (p. 230).

Hardy's use of irony can range from this tangled and complex effect to a simpler form of verbal irony. One fine example of this is provided by the remarks of Christopher Coney about Farfrae in chapter VIII. Having heard Farfrae sing his romantic songs about

Scotland, Coney asks, 'What did ye come away from yer own country for, young maister, if ye be so wownded about it?'

The fact that we can so readily find instances of irony within the 'rustic' levels of Casterbridge society as well as in the higher reaches amply demonstrates the pervasive force and influence of this device. Be sure to take careful note of those many examples. Their cumulative effect creates the tragic feeling of the novel.

AGRICULTURE: OLD WAYS AND NEW

Farming permeates *The Mayor of Casterbridge*. The Henchard we first meet is a nameless labourer characterized by his working clothes and the tools of his trade. His twenty years of wealth are founded on agriculture. It is as a peasant and bitter philosopher we see him at the end, thinking about the ironies of Fate 'as his hay-knife crunched down among the sweet-smelling grassy stems'. Throughout, Caster-bridge itself is characterized as a farming town (pp. 94–6, 128–31) and many crucial moments centre around farming incidents or rustic holidays – the 'growed wheat', the arrival of a seed-drill, the valuing of a haystack, an agricultural fair or a celebration. Henchard's financial ruin is caused by a disastrous change in the weather, his suspicions of Farfrae and Lucetta are confirmed as they go to watch the moonlight harvesting.

All this is far more than picturesque, far more than Hardy's wish to be 'quaint' or 'olde-worlde'. Farming is a very physical activity, it is absolutely not a nine-to-five routine, above all it is a way of life completely at one with the forces of Nature. These are indifferent, even hostile. Hardy wants to show us man's place in the world and he does so against farming, mankind's most basic activity.

Henchard's financial ruin is the clearest example of the harshness of Nature towards man, even a man as full of energy and initiative as Henchard. Indeed, it is precisely these qualities of energy and in-itiative that make the struggle between man and Nature particularly dramatic. For Henchard is not yet a passive sufferer. He seizes on the chance to gamble with Nature directly. He buys up corn in the hope that the weather will change and that he will be able to sell his stock at a yet higher price. He fails. The weather changes only when it is far too late and Henchard is on the brink of bankruptcy. His wealth has come from agriculture but agriculture is largely at the mercy of natural forces. A man like Henchard may show initiative, exercise his will, but in the end Nature is indifferent, even hostile to his efforts. A man such as Henchard is not meant to be happy. He may try to exploit Nature through farming, for a time he may even be successful, but in the end the forces of Nature are against him.

Such, of course, is Hardy's major theme, what we may call his view of man's eternal predicament. However, Hardy also uses agriculture for something else: to show the old ways of life giving way to the new, successful, scientific ones. Henchard, when speculating on the price of wheat, goes to see a weather-prophet. This is no more than superstition. Farfrae, the modern man, relies on science. It is he who introduces the seed-drill which ensures no grain of wheat is wasted (p. 240). It is he who has a device for curing 'growed wheat' and so saves Henchard from great embarrassment. This difference of approach between the two men is crucial and it is made early on in the novel by Henchard himself (near the end of the chapter, p. 117):

In my business, 'tis true that strength and bussle build up a firm. But judgement and knowledge are what keep it established. Unluckily, I am bad at science, Farfrae; bad at figures – a rule o' thumb sort of man. You are just the reverse – I can see that. I have been looking for such as you these two year, and yet you are not for me.

Henchard is stormy, impulsive. Up to now he has carried all before him by sheer force of personality. But this is not enough. Such a man can indeed create a business, he can also destroy it. What he cannot do is conserve, maintain and carefully build. He will get swept up in the tides of his own emotion. This is made beautifully clear when Henchard returns from his dramatic reunion with Susan to find Farfrae sitting down doing the accounts (p. 146). Quite simply, Henchard is 'mentally and physically unfit for grubbing subtleties from soiled paper'. He is quite prepared to pay for a celebration out of his own pocket and this is an expansive, generous gesture. Unfortunately, the people prefer to go to Farfrae's celebration, even though they have to pay for it. Again, when Farfrae introduces the seed-drill to Casterbridge, both Lucetta and Elizabeth-Jane realize he is responsible for it. Farfrae is the man of progress and for Lucetta this certainly adds to his attractiveness.

But Elizabeth-Jane's response is important (p. 240). She sees how such mechanization destroys the poetry, the human feeling of farming. Farfrae, the man of progress, is not a man of deep emotion. He is not expansive, like Henchard, rather he is calculating in both senses of the word: he plans carefully and he is almost never betrayed by emotion. Hardy comments (end of the chapter, p. 294) that when Farfrae buys up Henchard's bankrupt business:

Thence forward the full sacks, looped with the shining chain, went scurrying up and down under the cathead, hairy arms were thrust out from the different door-ways, and the grain was hauled in; trusses of hay were tossed anew in and out of the barns, and the wimbles creaked; while the scales and steelyards began to be busy where guesswork had formerly been the rule.

This is the way that leads to the factory farm. But it should also be noticed that Farfrae drops his workers' wages by a shilling a week and that they do not resent this because life is now quieter, more regular: 'No busting out, no slamming of doors, no meddling with yer eternal soul and all that.'

Henchard is great to the extent that his passions are great. He has a hero's energy, a hero's ability to love and hate. He leads his life with a vigour and impulsiveness that are at once exciting and terrifying. They enrich but they destroy. In the end they destroy Henchard himself. He loses everything. Most tragically, perhaps, he loses his great power to recreate himself. He runs out of 'zest' (p. 395). Farfrae, newly rich, calculating and slightly smug, wins virtually everything. With such a man, ordinary life is possible. His labourers are the first to appreciate this. What he cannot have – what his emotional blandness spares him – is the fullness of Henchard's tragic vision. As a man, the penniless Henchard, humbled by the forces of Nature and

his own temperament, is grander than Farfrae for all his pile of gold.
It is right that Henchard should wish to be namelessly hidden in the
earth which he exploited and which helped to bring him low. He
starts and ends the novel as a nameless peasant, a man of the soil.

A NOTE ON THE CORN LAWS

In the 'Author's Preface' (p. 67), Hardy makes the point that in
reading his novel we have 'to bear in mind that, in the days recalled
by the tale, the home Corn Trade, *on which so much of the action turns*
[my italics], had an importance that can hardly be realized by those
accustomed to the sixpenny loaf of the present date and to the present
indifference of the public to harvest weather'.

The book was completed in 1885, but its action is set soon after the
Napoleonic Wars which ended in 1815. This was significant in relation
to the economy of this country. In time of war, a great deal of
emphasis is placed on the provision of food. Imports from abroad are
made difficult and so countries have to become more self-reliant.
The harvests of 1813 and 1814 were particularly good. And the end
of the war meant that importing of wheat once again became a
possibility. The sudden generous supply of wheat available brought
the price down so low that farmers were threatened with bankruptcy.
The reality of this situation is evident at the beginning of *The Mayor
of Casterbridge* where work on the land is becoming more and more
difficult to find. Henchard, a skilled hay-trusser, is finding it difficult
to get work, and a turnip-hoer gives an indication of a drift from the
fields and the countryside where 'the volk [had] nowhere to go'
(p. 71).

In the 1815 Parliament the landowners introduced a Corn Law
which would fix the lowest selling price of corn. It was decided that
eighty shillings a quarter was the price that would provide the farmer
with at least some reasonable reward. Imports of corn were stopped
whenever the selling price fell below this eighty shilling mark. This
was not altogether effective from the landowners' point of view

because the price of corn was not kept up to eighty shillings. However, government ministers did make some provision to protect the landlords' interests. A sliding scale of prices was introduced to help make the importing of corn more difficult. The landlords prospered. The price of corn began to rise in 1823 and the lack of foreign competition meant that a corn-merchant could grow rapidly rich. This lack of competition from abroad shows why Henchard is anxious when he suddenly finds competition too close to home in the shape of Donald Farfrae. It also shows why the new mechanical aids mean so much to Donald Farfrae. And, finally, it shows us how Donald was able so quickly 'to pile for him a large heap of gold where a little one had been' (p. 264).

Glossary

Abrahamic success: Abraham was called 'the father of the Jewish nation' and had hundreds of children

Achilles: famous Greek hero who, in Greek mythology, was trained by a centaur to hunt

Adonis: the beautiful youth loved by Aphrodite in Greek legend

Adullam: a Biblical place name referring to a resort of those in distress

Aeolian: as though from an Aeolian harp: wire strings were strung between the branches of trees; the wind would create music by playing through the wires

Akin to a coach: Elizabeth-Jane realizes that she may have the chance of riding in the mayoral coach

Alastor: an avenging god in Greek mythology

Ancient rummers: large glasses

Animalcules: animals

Antipodean absences: reference to the transportation of convicts to Australia

Antiquated slop: a rather indelicate way of referring to the age of the furmity that is being served

Aphrodite: the Greek goddess of love

Apollo and Diana: in Greek mythology they were the gods of sun and moon

Apostle, the weak: Peter who denied Christ (see Matthew xxvi: 73)

Apotheosis: since she had become privileged

Argus eyes: in Greek legend Argus had a hundred eyes. When he was killed they were transferred to the peacock's feathers by the goddess Juno

Arthur's Seat: a beauty spot high above Edinburgh

As lief not: rather not

Ashlar: of squared stones

Assize town: a town where major trials were held

Attenuated: thinned out

Austerlitz: the greatest victory of Napoleon (1769–1821) was gained here in 1805

Ballet: ballad

Banded teetotaller: belongs to a group which avoids alcohol

Barley-mow: stack of sheaves of corn

Baruch: a Hebrew poet in the Old Testament

Bass-viols: cellos

Be honeycombed: to clean out

Be jowned: damn it!

Bellerophon: a hero of Greek legend who killed his brother; the story is told in the *Iliad*

Bents: reeds

Bethesda: a reference to a miracle healing in a town of that name in the New Testament (John v: 7)

Bibbing: drinking

Bide where you be: stay where you are

Bloody warriers: wall flowers

Blower: the metal plate in a fireplace to

help provide a draught to draw the fire upwards

Boldwood: a gentleman farmer who is one of the main characters in Hardy's novel *Far From the Madding Crowd*

Botany Bay: the Australian destination to which transported convicts were sent

Brick-nogging: describes the way in which houses were built of timber with bricks between instead of plaster

Brine ... green wound: salt on a fresh wound

Brougham: a small carriage drawn by one horse

Bruckle: rough and ready

Butter-firkins: casks in which butter was stored after being salted

Cain: son of Adam and Eve in the Old Testament who, because of his murder of his brother, Abel, was doomed to wander the earth (see Genesis iv: 13)

Cake-dough: she'll wish her position could be reversed

Calico: cotton cloth

Calphurnia: the wife of Julius Caesar who tried to warn him of the dangers to his life on the day of his murder

Candle snuff: a metal hood used to extinguish candles

Candlemas: 2 February, a feast of Our Lady

Capharnaum: Christ spoke of this place on the Sea of Galilee as 'a land where death overshadowed' men. Hardy suggests that this was exactly the experience of Elizabeth-Jane

Capitol: the reference is to the place of government of ancient Rome

Carking: troublesome

Carpet-bag: a travelling bag made of carpet material

Cathead: a beam projecting from the roof over which run pulley and tackle for lifting heavy loads

Centrifugal: flying away from the centre

Centripetal: moving towards the centre

Chagrin: anger

Champaign: countryside

Chancel: the eastern part of a church reserved for the clergy

Chap o' wax: a man whose future seems perfect (a reference to a wax-work here in which all parts are judged to be perfect)

Chaps: cheeks

Charing Cross: central London railway station

Chassez-dechassez: going to and fro, in and out

Chaw: chew

Cherubims warble: wordless

Chimbley: chimney

Chippendale and Sheraton: the reference is to the furniture designed by Thomas Chippendale (1718–79) and Thomas Sheraton (1751–1806)

Claning: cleaning

Clime: the rim of wood round the bottom of the barrel

Clue line: a kind of guide-line – the term is taken from sailing

Coliseum: famous monument in Rome where Christians were sacrificed

Comminatory: threatening

Commissioners: these operated like the Official Receiver in modern bankruptcies

Comus: a masque by John Milton (1608–74)

Concatenation of events: a chain of linked happenings

Concatenations of phenomena: a chain of unusual events

Confound: ruin

Congeries: collections

Constantine: the name of thirteen Roman emperors who reigned between 306 and 1453

Contrarious: opposed

Coomb: small valley

Coopers: barrel-makers

Copyholders: those with no deeds to a house or land but only a copy of the court role

Corregio (1494–1534): Antonio Corregio, an Italian Renaissance painter

Corren: corn

Cortege: procession

Coulter: blade of a plough

Cow barton: cattle-yard

Coxcomb: a conceited fool

Crock: pot

Crouds: crude fiddles

Crusoe: character in the novel *Robinson Crusoe*, by Daniel Defoe (1661–1731)

Cursory: brief

Cust polls: cursed heads

Cust: cursed

Cyma-recta curve: with a concave curve

Dan Cupid: Cupid is the god of love – Dan is an archaic term for 'Master'

David: eleventh-century (B.C.) King of Israel, who wrote the Psalms (elsewhere referred to as the Psalmist)

Daze me: damn me

Deal wand: a stick made from fir wood

Denizens: inhabitants

Diana Multimammia: many-breasted Diana: the Greek goddess of fertility

Diment: diamond

Dimity: cotton fabric

Dirk: dagger

Disappeared for a time: went to prison!

Dog days: the hottest days of summer

Dogged: determined

Doggery: tricks

Domiciliation: house, shelter

Doxology: he really means theology

Drag: heavy weight on a cart that acted as a brake

Dramless: without a drink (or dram, measure of drink)

Drop: reference to a public hanging

Dungmixen: dunghill

Earthwork: remains of Roman or prehistoric camp

Eclat: lustre, glow

Elizabethan gables: end of the building done in Tudor style

Emmaus: it was here that, according to the Gospel of Luke xxiv: 13–35, the risen Christ appeared to two of his disciples

Emolliated: softened

Enervated: lacking energy

Enfilading: threading through

Ephemeral: passing, fleeting

Espaliers: fruit trees trained to climb a fence

Evil: Scrofula (often known as 'the king's evil') which was supposed to be cured by the touch of a king's hand

Exacerbated: made worse, tortured

Extenuation: excuse

Fabrication: lie

Façade: external appearance (usually of a building)

Fall: veil

Felloe: the rim of the wheel

Felo de se: suicide

Festoons: drooping chains of flowers and garlands, used for decoration

Fête carillonnée: a festival of bell ringing

Fetichistic: Hardy is suggesting that his attention was a superstitious kind of obsession

Fiasco: disaster

Field flagons: large vessels containing beer used for carrying to the fields for thirsty labourers

Fifth instinct: really 'fifth instant' (an

example of the abuse of English by Stubberd)

Filial: like a son/daughter

Fillip: stimulus (usually used in a positive sense, but here is, ironically, negative)

Finesse: niceties, skill

Finnikin: trifling (to him)

Flail and winnowing fan: reference to tools and instruments used for dealing with corn and grain

Flexuous: bending, twisting

Flock bed: a mattress filled with wool-remnants

Fly: a light carriage

Fond: foolish

Friable: easily crumbling

Frothing measures: pints of ale with frothy heads

Furlough: leave granted to the military

Furmity: wheat boiled in milk

Fustian: cotton cloth of coarse texture

Gaberlunzie: a travelling beggar

Galvanized into spasmodic movements: a reference to the story of Frankenstein, by Mary Shelley (1797–1851)

Gawk-hammer: stupid

Gazebo: a tower or viewing balcony

Georgian: architecture associated with the eighteenth century

Gibbous: hump-backed and rounded

Giddying worm: a worm that causes sheep to become giddy and die

Gigs: carriages

Goblin Page: a dwarf in the *Lay of the Last Minstrel*, by Sir Walter Scott (1771–1832)

Gothic: architecture of the medieval period

Grog: beer

Ground figures: pictures of people etched in the glass

Growed wheat: wheat that had sprouted before it was harvested

Gurth's collar of brass: a swine-herd in the novel *Ivanhoe*, by Sir Walter Scott; Gurth, as a serf, had to wear a brass collar

Hadrian: Roman emperor (A.D. 76–138) who built the wall in the north of England to keep out Picts and Scots

Hairguard: cloth used for covering pocket-watches

Hannah Dominy: anno domini (in the year of our Lord)

Harlequinade: part of a pantomime in which a harlequin plays a large part

Harum-scarum: not having any cares

Hawkers: general term for traders

Heptarchy: the seven kingdoms of Anglo-Saxon Britain

Hiring fair: a fair or market where workers offered themselves for hire

Holland: a linen fabric

Hontish: proud

Humstrums: improvised instruments

Hyperborean: from the far north

Idiosyncrasy: odd habit

In the interim: in the meanwhile

Incipient: beginning, the onset

Indigence: poverty

Intimate: became lovers

Iron-dogs: the iron bars of a fire basket, often called andirons

Jacob: a Biblical character, a patriarch, son of Isaac and Rebecca. He is to be found in the Book of Genesis

Jamb: side post of a doorway or window

Jints: joints, parts of the body

Job: an Old Testament prophet afflicted by God

Joseph: a Biblical character in the Old Testament noted most for his interpretation of dreams and for his rejection by his many brothers

Josephus: a Jewish historian (A.D. 37–100) whose *History of the Jews* was popular in nineteenth-century England

Jotuns: giants of Scandinavian mythology

Journeymen: workers hired by the day

Jovial Jews: a reference to the Biblical incident where the Jews drank to excess (see Exodus xxxii: 19)

Jumps: underclothes

Karnac: ancient ruins of Thebes on the Nile

Keacorn: throat

Kerseymere: fine woollen cloth

Kits: miniature violins

Knee-naps: pads for the knees

Laconism: brevity of speech

Lammigers: cripples

Land smuggler: receiver of stolen goods

Laocoön: a Trojan priest who, according to Greek myth, was crushed to death with his sons by two serpents

Larry: disturbance, commotion

Le Rochefoucauld: French philosopher (1613–80)

Leery: tired and hungry

Liege subjects . . . : Hardy is suggesting Englishmen were very insular

Life holders: those who held a lease on land or house lasting for several generations

Like Ashton . . . Ravenswood: in Sir Walter Scott's novel *The Bride of Lammermore* Ashton watches Ravenswood vanish in a quicksand

List at the bottom: the dough had not risen and so the bread had a thick bottom layer

Lucifer: refers to the planet Venus, the morning star

Lucubrations: night-time studies

Mai Dun: Maiden Castle near Dorchester

Malignant star: fate

Malter's: a malster, a malt-maker

Martinmas or *Martin's Day:* this occurs on 11 November; here it refers to a sudden show of warmth

Mattock: a kind of tool shaped like a pick at one end and a chisel shape at the other

Mien: appearance revealing a mood

Mind: remember

Minerva: the Greek goddess of wisdom and craftsmen

Miserables: poor and destitute people

Modus vivendi: way of life

Monolithic: pillars of stone

Motley: mixed

Muff: an article of clothing, usually of fur, used to keep hands warm

Mullioned: a Gothic effect where windows were divided by vertical stonework

Narrowly: closely

Nathan: a Jewish prophet who had the courage to accuse King David of a great crime and persuade him to repent

Netting: needlework

Nettled: the sense of being stung or hurt

Nimbus: a kind of atmosphere, a cloud, an aura. The term is being used here quite ironically

Node (of all orbits): central point

Novalis: a German poet, real name Baron Friedrich von Hardenburg (1772–1801)

Numerical fogs: problems caused for him by numbers

Off-gig lamp: lamp on the off-side of a carriage

Omniverously: hungrily devouring everything

Other fish to fry: other business on hand

Oven pyle: a shovel for putting loaves into the oven and pulling them out

Ovid: Roman poet (43 B.C.–A.D. 18) whose poem *Metamorphoses* is used here for reference. The line quoted means 'I can see what is the better way, and can agree with it; but I follow what is less desirable'

Padan-Aram: the Syrian desert where Jacob worked for his uncle Laban caring for his sheep

Palladian: classical Roman architecture made popular in 'modern' times by Andraea Palladio (1518–80), an Italian architect

Pantomimic: as in a pantomime where the actors would assume exaggerated poses

Pari passu: at an equal rate of progress

Pattens: wooden overshoes for rough weather

Pembroke tables: tables with drop leaves and a drawer, dating from the eighteenth century

People full of reciprocity: people who are ready to exchange views

Perambulatory term: refers to the expression 'walking out together'

Peremptory: sudden and dramatic

Petty Sessions: courts where minor offences are tried by magistrates

Pharaohs: rulers of Egypt in Biblical times

Pier glass: a long mirror placed between two windows

Pier: a pillar

Pile: a collection of ruins

Pillow: pillar

Pinched, blasted, snuffed: diseased

Piquant: having an invigorating effect

Pis aller: the last resort

Pitching: the tar or pitch that lined barrels and made them air-tight

Pixy-ring: rings of toadstools (supposed to be magic)

Plim: swell up

Plumb-straight: phrase taken from the plumb-line used for accuracy of level and direction

Poils: heads

Prester John: an Ethiopian emperor who, according to legend, was punished by the gods for wanting to add Paradise to his lands

Primed with a spoon: having a spoon in it

Princess Ida: the leading character in the poem *The Princess*, by Tennyson (1809–92)

Pristine: as they first were

Prophet's chamber: a reference to the room prepared for the prophet Elisha in an incident in the Book of Kings in the Old Testament

Protean: assuming different shapes and forms – the reference is taken from the name Proteus, the mythical man of the sea who could change shape at will

Psalmist: a reference to the writer of the Psalms, King David

Puffings: clothes with plenty of decoration

Purl of waters: bubbling of the river

Purlieu: area, environment

Quacks: persons pretending to be doctors and offering patent cures and medicines

Quag: a mess, a lot of trouble

Quarter-barrel: a barrel containing nine gallons of ale

Quickset: hawthorn hedge

Ramifications: various paths, tracks

Randy: celebration

Rantipole rubbish: rude songs

Rape-seed: a turnip-type crop used for feeding sheep

Recantation: expression of regret, repentance

Recent poet: probably a reference to William Wordsworth (1770–1850)

Refluent: throwing back

Rencounter: casual meeting

Reticulated: lined

Reverie: daydream

Reviviscent: reawakening

Ring, the: a Roman arena used at one time for combat

Ringstaked-and-spotted: a reference to the inferior cattle given to Jacob by Laban

Roast Beef of Old England: a popular song

Roasting ... waxen image/stirring ... brew: these were spells to bring bad luck

Rogue's march: the march-tune played when a soldier was dismissed from the service

Romans: here the reference is to Roman Catholics

Romeo: the hero of *Romeo and Juliet*

Rosalind: heroine of *As You Like It*

Rouge-et-noir: red and black

Roysterers: revellers

Rub: difficulty

Sacrarium: sanctuary

Sallows: willow trees

Samson: a Jewish hero who was distinguished for his great strength – this was seen to lodge in his hair of which he was 'shorn'!

Sanguinary: bloody

Saul at his reception by Samuel: this incident is to be found in the Old Testament Book of Samuel, and tells of the meeting between the future king of Israel, Saul, and the prophet Samuel

Schiedam: Holland gin

Schwarwasser: black water

Seed lip: sower's basket

Seines: fishing nets

Sensational exits: reference to executions

Sequestrated: confiscated, taken away

Sequestration: isolation

Serpentining: wandering, winding

Serpent: a long bass wind instrument

Settles: benches

Seven Sleepers: a reference to seven Christians who, during the Roman persecution, hid in a cave in Ephesus. They are reputed to have slept there for, some say, over 300 years, others for just under 200 years

Shade ... upthrown: a quotation from the poem *The Revolt of Islam*, by Shelley (1792–1821)

Shallow and Silence: two magistrates in *Henry IV, Part 2*

Shambles: slaughter-house

Shocks: sheaves of corn

Shoon: shoes

Shorn: deprived

Sicilian Mariners' Hymn: a tune popular at the time to which Psalm 19 was sung

Skellintons: skeletons

Skimmity-ride: this is a 'skimmington-ride' – a show to shame adulterers whose effigies were paraded through town

Slatterns: women who dressed in a careless and slovenly fashion

Sniff and snuff: allowing attention

Socked: gasped

Soi-disant: calling herself

Solicitus timor: anxious fear

Some falls by the wayside ... thorns: a reference to Christ's parable of the sower in Matthew xiii: 4–7

Sotto voce: in a whisper

Soughed: sighed

Soujtron: southern

Spencer: close-fitting jacket

Spirituous: alcoholic

Spit: headland

Spittoon: a vessel into which one spat

Springes: traps

St Helier: chief Jersey town

Staylace dealer: a woman who sold lace

for undergarments: 'stays', sometimes called corsets

Stint of reciprocal feeling: Lucetta was not returning Henchard's warmth

Stoically: showing great endurance without signs of emotion

Stone saddles: raised platforms of stone

Stone-crop: a yellow-flowered herb

Stunpoll: a stupid man

Subscription: signature

Superciliously: in a sneering fashion

Superficies: external appearances

Supinely extended: lying on her back

Suppliant: a person who begs

Swingels: the swinging part of a flail

Swipes: diluted beer

Sylph: spirit of the air

Tailing: substandard corn

Tamurlaine: the Mongolian conqueror whose army used seven-foot long trumpets

Taper and wax: the heat of the lighted taper would melt the wax which would then seal the letter

Taties: potatoes

Terpsichorean: dance steps: Terpsichore was the Greek muse of song and dance

Thames tunnel ... toys of yore: looking like the Thames tunnel as seen in peep-shows, popular at the time

Thill horse: horse between shafts

Thimble-riggers: cheats and tricksters who used the pea-and-cup trick. Clients are asked to bet where the pea is

Till the great trumpet: a reference to the Last Day, Judgement Day

Tilt bonnets: hats 'tilted' to keep out the sun

Titian: a Renaissance painter from Venice (1490–1576)

To go snacks wi' en: marry (literally, share his food)

To the zero: in close imitation of

Toad-bags: bags, containing legs torn from a toad, which were worn as good-luck charms

Topography: detailed description of the environment

Toppered: toppled, overcame

Toss-pots: drunkards

Tracery, jambs, arch-labels: architectural terms referring to features of windows and doors

Transfixture: rooting, to the spot

Transubstantiated: changed his very nature

Tudor arch: an arch formed with four arcs (the style belongs to the late medieval period)

Tumuli: burial mounds

Turmit head: turnip head, idiot

Twanking: moaning

Twelve-bushel strength: strong beer

Tyro: a novice

Undulatory: lilting

Unicorn: the mythological animal shown on the Royal Coat of Arms

Vagaries: efforts

Varden: farthing

'vation: abbreviation for 'salvation'

Ventricles: cavities (relating here to the heart)

Via: Roman road

Viands: food

Victorine: a lady's fur scarf, fastened at the neck

Vitrified: glazed (by the sun)

Viva voce: by word of mouth

Wagon-tilts: canvas tops of wagons

Wambled: staggered

Wambling: wandering

Wanton hussies: amoral women

Wash: the pig food

Water-tights: wellington boots

Weal: well-being

Welkin: the sky

Weltlust: love of worldly things

Where the clouds drop fatness: a quotation from Psalm v: 11

Whole Duty of Man: a moral book popular at the time, first published in 1658

Whose gestures ... mind: reference to Shelley's poem *The Revolt of Islam*

Whose roof trees had fallen: who had lost their houses

Wicket: gate

Wimble: a tool used for twisting the material that kept the hay together

Wimbling: threading or tying

Wise in her generation: a reference to Christ's parable recorded in Luke xvi: 1–13, of the shrewd steward who cheated his master

With terminative emphasis: with such stress as to suggest the end of the conversation

Withy basket: a basket made of willow branches

Worm i' the bud: a reference to a disease in the rose that eats it away

Wowned: wounded

Wraith: a person's double

Yahoo: the word implies brutes and is taken from the novel *Gulliver's Travels*, by Jonathan Swift (1667–1745)

Yard of Clay: long-stemmed clay pipe

You mun: you must

You take time by the forelock: you hurry things up!

Zilver-snuffers: silver objects used to put out candles

Zwailing: wandering around aimlessly

Examination Questions

1. 'Farfrae's character was just the reverse of Henchard's.' Give an account of (*a*) the episode involving Abel Whittle and his lateness in arriving at work, and (*b*) one other episode involving Henchard and Farfrae. In each case point out the contrast in character between Henchard and Farfrae.

(*Joint Matriculation Board, 1978*)

2. It has been said that Elizabeth-Jane is the most admirable character in the book. Describe her character, pointing out those features that seem to justify this statement, and indicate any aspects of her character that you find less attractive. Refer to the novel to support your ideas.

(*Joint Matriculation Board, 1978*)

3. Examine closely the contrasting characters of Henchard and Farfrae and the development of the relationship between them.

(*Joint Matriculation Board, 1980*)

4. Discuss Hardy's portrayal of women in *The Mayor of Casterbridge*.

(*Joint Matriculation Board, 1980*)

5. 'Henchard is a victim of his own temperament and follies.' To what extent do you consider this to be true?

(*Associated Examining Board*)

6. At the end of the novel, Hardy draws our attention to the 'persistence of the unseen'. Show the workings of this 'persistence' in Elizabeth-Jane's life.

(*Associated Examining Board*)

7. Contrast the attitudes to Elizabeth-Jane of Henchard and Newson.

(*Associated Examining Board*)

8. Illustrate the way in which Hardy makes his description of place important to the action of the novel by detailed discussion of two localities.

(*Associated Examining Board*)

9. 'It is not loss of wealth which is Henchard's supreme tragedy, but isolation and loss of self-esteem.' How far do you agree?

(*Associated Examining Board*)

10. Choose *two* of the poor people who are the minor characters in this novel and say what part each of them plays in the story.

(*Associated Examining Board*)

11. Several characters in *The Mayor of Casterbridge* experience reversals of fortune. Choose two such incidents each involving different characters, and compare the ways in which each is affected by what happens.

(*Associated Examining Board*)

12. What does the character of Lucetta contribute to the novel?

(*Associated Examining Board*)

13. How does Henchard's relationship with Lucetta differ from that with Susan? What different qualities are brought out in him by the women?

(Associated Examining Board)

14. For which character in the novel do you feel most pity? Refer closely to the novel in accounting for your choice.

(Associated Examining Board)

15. At one point in the novel Hardy claims 'Character is Fate'. What characteristics of Henchard can be seen as responsible for his fate?

(Associated Examining Board)

16. By specific reference to incidents in the novel examine the part played by the weather in *The Mayor of Casterbridge*.

(Associated Examining Board)

17. What initially attracted Henchard to Farfrae? What were the major contributory factors in their eventual rift?

(Associated Examining Board)

18. Examine the part played in the novel by (*a*) Jopp, (*b*) Abel Whittle.

(Associated Examining Board)

19. 'Character is Fate' writes Hardy. Briefly explain what you think he means by this, and then say how far you think Henchard's fate is determined by his character.

(Cambridge Local Examination Board, 1977)

20. 'Susan, Farfrae, Lucetta, Elizabeth-Jane all had gone from him, one after one, either by his fault or by his misfortune.' Select *two* of these characters and make clear how far Henchard had lost them by his fault and how far by his misfortune.

(*Cambridge Local Examination Board*)

21. Show that Hardy's minor characters not only assist with the development of the plot but also add to our enjoyment of the novel.

(*Cambridge Local Examination Board*)

FOR THE BEST IN PAPERBACKS, LOOK FOR THE

In every corner of the world, on every subject under the sun, Penguins represent quality and variety – the very best in publishing today.

For complete information about books available from Penguin and how to order them, write to us at the appropriate address below. Please note that for copyright reasons the selection of books varies from country to country.

In the United Kingdom: For a complete list of books available from Penguin in the U.K., please write to *Dept EP, Penguin Books Ltd, Harmondsworth, Middlesex, UB7 0DA*

In the United States: For a complete list of books available from Penguin in the U.S., please write to *Dept BA, Viking Penguin, 299 Murray Hill Parkway, East Rutherford, New Jersey 07073*

In Canada: For a complete list of books available from Penguin in Canada, please write to *Penguin Books Canada Limited, 2801 John Street, Markham, Ontario L3R 1B4*

In Australia: For a complete list of books available from Penguin in Australia, please write to the *Marketing Department, Penguin Books Australia Ltd, P.O. Box 257, Ringwood, Victoria 3134*

In New Zealand: For a complete list of books available from Penguin in New Zealand, please write to the *Marketing Department, Penguin Books (N.Z.) Ltd, Private Bag, Takapuna, Auckland 9*

In India: For a complete list of books available from Penguin in India, please write to *Penguin Overseas Ltd, 706 Eros Apartments, 56 Nehru Place, New Delhi 110019*

FOR THE BEST IN PAPERBACKS, LOOK FOR THE

PENGUIN PASSNOTES

This comprehensive series, designed to help O-level and CSE students, includes:

SUBJECTS
Biology
Chemistry
Economics
English Language
French
Geography
Human Biology
Mathematics
Modern Mathematics
Modern World History
Narrative Poems
Physics

SHAKESPEARE
As You Like It
Henry IV, Part I
Henry V
Julius Caesar
Macbeth
The Merchant of Venice
A Midsummer Night's Dream
Romeo and Juliet
Twelfth Night

LITERATURE
Arms and the Man
Cider With Rosie
Great Expectations
Jane Eyre
Kes
Lord of the Flies
A Man for All Seasons
The Mayor of Casterbridge
My Family and Other Animals
Pride and Prejudice
The Prologue to The Canterbury
    Tales
Pygmalion
Saint Joan
She Stoops to Conquer
Silas Marner
To Kill a Mockingbird
War of the Worlds
The Woman in White
Wuthering Heights

FOR THE BEST IN PAPERBACKS, LOOK FOR THE 🐧

PENGUIN DICTIONARIES

Archaeology

Architecture

Art and Artists

Biology

Botany

Building

Chemistry

Civil Engineering

Commerce

Computers

Decorative Arts

Design and Designers

Economics

English and European
  History

English Idioms

Geography

Geology

Historical Slang

Literary Terms

Mathematics

Microprocessors

Modern History 1789–1945

Modern Quotations

Physical Geography

Physics

Political Quotations

Politics

Proverbs

Psychology

Quotations

Religions

Saints

Science

Sociology

Surnames

Telecommunications

The Theatre

Troublesome Words

Twentieth Century History

Dictionaries of all these – and more – in Penguin

PENGUIN MODERN CLASSICS

The Glass Bead Game   Hermann Hesse

In a perfect world where passions are tamed by meditation, where academic discipline and order are paramount, scholars, isolated from hunger, family, children and women, play the ultra-aesthetic glass bead game. This is Hesse's great novel, which has made a significant contribution to contemporary philosophic literature.

If It Die   André Gide

A masterpiece of French prose, *If It Die* is Gide's record of his childhood, his friendships, his travels, his sexual awakening and, above all, the search for truth which characterizes his whole life and all his writing.

Dark as the Grave wherein my Friend is Laid   Malcolm Lowry

A Dantean descent into hell, into the infernal landscape of Mexico, the same Mexico as Lowry's *Under the Volcano*, a country of mental terrors and spiritual chasms.

The Collected Short Stories   Katherine Mansfield

'She could discern in a trivial event or an insignificant person some moving revelation or motive or destiny . . . There is an abundance of that tender and delicate art which penetrates the appearances of life to discover the elusive causes of happiness and grief' – W. E. Williams in his Introduction to *The Garden Party and Other Stories*

Sanctuary   William Faulkner

Faulkner draws America's Deep South exactly as he saw it: seething with life and corruption; and *Sanctuary* asserts itself as a compulsive and unsparing vision of human nature.

The Expelled and Other Novellas   Samuel Beckett

Rich in verbal and situational humour, the four stories in this volume offer the reader a fascinating insight into Beckett's preoccupation with the helpless individual consciousness, a preoccupation which has remained constant throughout Beckett's work.

THE LIBRARY OF EVERY CIVILIZED PERSON

Netochka Nezvanova Fyodor Dostoyevsky

Dostoyevsky's first book tells the story of 'Nameless Nobody' and introduces many of the themes and issues which will dominate his great masterpieces.

Selections from the Carmina Burana A verse translation by David Parlett

The famous songs from the *Carmina Burana* (made into an oratorio by Carl Orff) tell of lecherous monks and corrupt clerics, drinkers and gamblers, and the fleeting pleasures of youth.

Fear and Trembling Søren Kierkegaard

A profound meditation on the nature of faith and submission to God's will which examines with startling originality the story of Abraham and Isaac.

Selected Prose Charles Lamb

Lamb's famous essays (under the strange pseudonym of Elia) on anything and everything have long been celebrated for their apparently innocent charm; this major new edition allows readers to discover the darker and more interesting aspects of Lamb.

The Picture of Dorian Gray Oscar Wilde

Wilde's superb and macabre novella, one of his supreme works, is reprinted here with a masterly Introduction and valuable Notes by Peter Ackroyd.

A Treatise of Human Nature David Hume

A universally acknowledged masterpiece by 'the greatest of all British Philosophers' – A. J. Ayer

PENGUIN CLASSICS

THE LIBRARY OF EVERY CIVILIZED PERSON